Praise for the Work of Jason Adam Sheets

"Alchemical and transformative, rooted deep in mystical traditions, these poems see and ask to be seen...Read [these poems] again and again."
– Janet Sylvester, author of *And Not to Break*

"If poetry is religion, [Sheets' poetry] is a sanctuary; a temple in which Sheets guides us to the altar. He gives us room enough to worship, seek absolution, or call forth ecstatic visions. Throughout he tries on the cloak of monk, prophet, and shaman, before settling effortlessly into the mantle of modern mystic. All of this feels as deliberate as the intricacies of each work...[it] casts us in shadow, gibbous ray, then maximum incandescence."
– Claudine Cain, *Black Elephant Lit*

"Like reading through a dream."
– Ryann Crofoot

"I felt alive with every word, every sentence that I read. Mesmerising, lyrical poetry bursting with emotions intertwined in creativity, at the seams. Raw, original, sophisticated, and yet the poetry rings with such candour. The writing style seems like that of the Romantic poets and offers a magical escape, a surreal transportation to our imaginations."
– Shelley D.

"Ethereal, has a life-altering impact."
– Korynne Michele

"[Sheets' poetry] reads like the description of a dream in free verse. It's almost as if someone tried to make poetry out of a surrealist painting."
– Andreea Martin, *Infinite Text Journal*

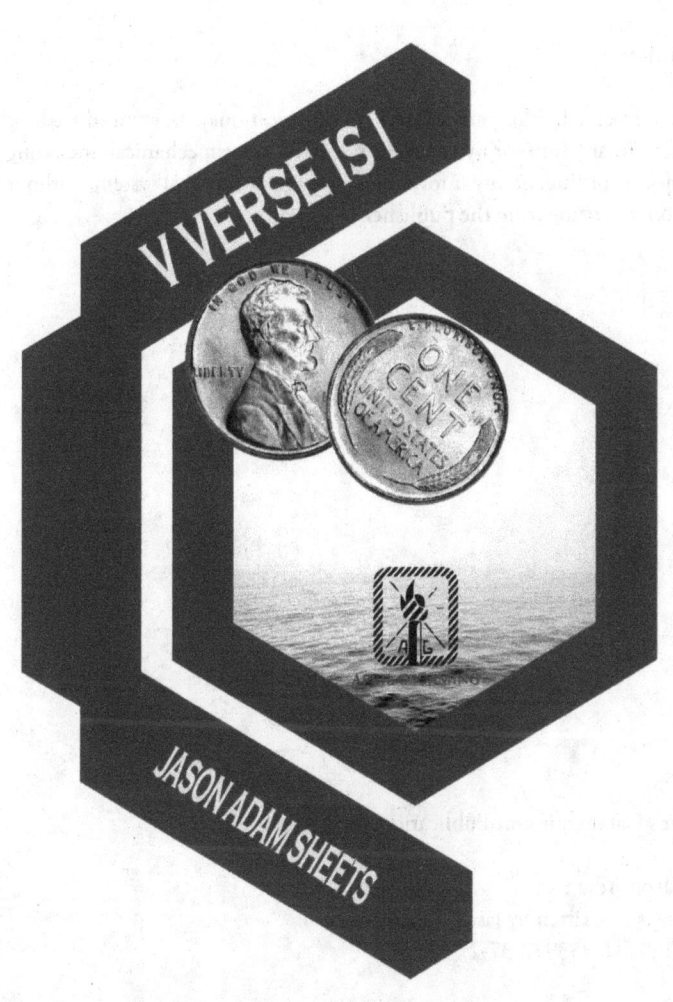

V VERSE IS I

JASON ADAM SHEETS

©2025 Jason Adam Sheets
Cover ©2025 Robyn Leigh Lear

-First Edition

Publisher's Cataloguing-in-Publication Data

Sheets, Jason Adam
    V verse is i / written by Jason Adam Sheets
    ISBN: 978-1-953932-37-2

1. Poetry: American - General 2. Literary Criticism: Poetry 3. Literary Criticism: Subjects & Themes - Religion I. Title II. Author

Library of Congress Control Number: 2025934712

Contents

NARRATIVES

SCHOLARLY CRITIQUES

I had never known of my Great Uncle Tommy, or much of my Appalachian lineage, until the year of this writing, at 41. I had no idea I shared blood with another poet, let alone one who attended a divinity school to study theology like I had. Although I knew that most on my father's side played music and wrote songs, when it came to poetry, education, and spiritual pursuits, I thought I was the only one like me in my family.

How extraordinary it is to discover these things about ourselves along the way, how Spirit truly does live in our blood . . .

Rev. Thomas T. May was born in 1919 in Pike County, Kentucky. He was a poet with a Doctor of Divinity Degree who preached throughout Kentucky for roughly fifty years. His great-grandfather—my great-great-grandfather—was Rev. Basil Hatfield, of the famed Hatfield-McCoy feud. Thomas T. May's book of poetry, *People and Poems*, was self-published through Brentwood Christian Press in 1991. *People and Poems* is comprised of dedications to family and friends, ruminations on being a pastor, and experiences while serving as a tank driver in World War II.

In the foreword to his book, Great Uncle Tommy writes: "Most of my poems are so personal and primitive that I am embarrassed to offer them for public consumption . . . Nevertheless, with such motivation as herein indicated, and with that subtle and secret inner longing of every would-be-writer—to be heard, to be read, to be recognized in any measure! I launch this little trial balloon." I hear you, dear brother. I often say the same about my own poems. So it goes . . .

I dedicate this book to my great uncle Tommy,
better known as Rev. Thomas T. May.

The Poetics of Homelessness

A Harvard graduate's reflections on being unhoused

After publication of the May-June 2024 feature "The Homelessness Public Health Crisis," Harvard Magazine received an email from Jason Adam Sheets, M.T.S. '21. A Pushcart Prize-nominated poet and essayist, Sheets earned a B.F.A. from Goddard College in Vermont and studied theopoetics at Harvard Divinity School (HDS). He has written three books of poetry: A Madness of Blue Obsidian, The Hour Wasp, and Theopoetica: An Anthology (all from April Gloaming Publishing); a fourth book of poems will be published this year. He has taught English at the University of New Hampshire and currently teaches for the Poetry in America program, associated with the PBS series of the same name.

Sheets is also homeless. For most of 2023, he slept unsheltered; this year he has been "couch-hopping" with friends in Cambridge, since he still cannot afford a fixed address of his own. In his email, he explained that the stereotype of guaranteed wealth for Ivy League graduates doesn't always hold true: "If you enter poor, you leave poor," he wrote. Sheets grew up in Plymouth, Massachusetts, in a lower-income, single-parent household, and after working numerous jobs, including as a steersman on a lobster boat and a taxi driver, he enrolled in college [in 2014] at age 32. In 2019, he matriculated at HDS.

In this essay, Sheets reflects on his experience of homelessness, its meaning to him as a person and a poet, and its connection to the wider national crisis.

—The Editors [Harvard Magazine, June 18, 2024]

I cannot remember the exact moment I became homeless. There was not one definitive event that led to my having to sleep beside train tracks or on bathroom floors. I was simply too broke for too long and unable to secure decent-enough employment that could afford me stable housing. I kept trying to save but couldn't save enough, and before I knew it, I found myself outside one night, aimlessly walking with nowhere to go. Walking for hours each day, or night, has since become habit.

Years ago, I saw a raven for the first time. I was in Vermont attending my inaugural residency as a college undergraduate in a low-residency B.F.A. program in creative writing, four years before I received a full scholarship to study poetry at Harvard. We poets are drawn to crows and ravens, something about the magic in their mystery, so I had always hoped to encounter one. It was fitting that my first encounter occurred when I committed to pursue my calling. Hearing that deep musical caw evoked something within me, something about Emerson's "long winding train reaching back into eternity" coupled with the difficulty of having both roots *and* wings.

All of us walk on a ground of many worlds, and we live in a world of many dualities. As a poet, I have each foot planted in a different world, perpetually tasked with distilling the effable from the ineffable without weakening the energy of the encounter. In both of these worlds, though, I'm a homeless Harvard alum—a paradox to most.

Sleeping on gravel is insufferable, but I can tell you how to make a comfortable makeshift bed on it out of practically nothing. Building a fire in the rain by the beach is insufferable, but I can tell you how to build a fire that will create just enough smoke to deter the horseflies from biting you while not drawing the attention of patrol officers. Guarding one's belongings while homeless is insufferable, but I can tell you how to talk to the agitated drug addicts or untreated Cluster B personalities who fell through the cracks who won't leave you alone because of something you have that they want, as addiction and mental illness run rampant in the homeless community. (See Lydialyle Gibson's article "Academia's Absence from Homelessness" for more on this.)

A person's capacity for experiencing suffering is the same as a person's capacity for experiencing joy. As a poet, I find joy in words and symbols, and being homeless has gifted me with an abundance of both, which I keep in the front pocket of my life. I'm grateful for words such as *home-less*, *dis-placed*, and *mis-fortuned*. I thank these words, for in each of them, we find not only linguistic duality but the poetic duality—the poison and remedy of interpretation: in *homeless* we find *home*, in *displaced* we find *place*, and in our *misfortune*, we can find *fortune*. If it weren't for poetry, I know that the experience of homelessness would have long since rusted my psychological gears to a locked state.

On April 30, 2024, I stood outside the gates of Harvard Yard in front of the Smith Campus Center waiting for a man from the City of Cambridge Department of Human Services to arrive and hand me a Verification of Homelessness through the window of his white work van. He pulled up to the corner of Dunster and handed me the document. I thanked him, then carefully placed the piece of paper into my backpack, the same backpack I wore each day from 2019-2021 while at Harvard. Two years ago, I walked across a stage at the graduation exercise for the classes of 2020 and 2021 and shook the hand of the dean of my school as he handed me a large white envelope that symbolized the master's degree I'd earned. The envelope was empty. (We'd received our degrees in the mail a year earlier due to the COVID-19 lockdown.) When I returned to my friend's place in Harvard Square, I pulled the Verification of Homelessness from my bag, feeling utterly unsure about how I felt about it. After uploading the photo of it to the places I needed to submit it, I pondered what to do with it and, for a moment, thought of that large white envelope.

There are many myths and stereotypes about being a Harvard graduate, but the one I attempt to reckon with most is the one that presumes that no matter who you are and where you come from, if you hold a degree from Harvard, you are free from having to worry about things such as job security, money, available credit, etc.... This is wishful thinking, especially if you were raised in a check-to-check single-parent household and entered college as an adult FGLI (first-generation, lower-income) student.

The thing about matriculating at Harvard as a working-class person living check-to-check is that you'll still likely be a working-class person living check-to-check after you graduate, at least for a time, and typically for a longer time than most in your cohort. Like many post-COVID graduates, I've spent the past two years submitting countless application portfolios to talent-acquisition teams for positions in my field that, I feel, I'm well-qualified to interview for: research assistantships; instructorships in expository writing; publishing and editing positions; faculty assistantships, etc.—but I've yet to receive more than one invitation to interview. It's important to note, too, that minimum wage employers won't often hire those in my situation because they know we're overqualified for their positions and that we'll likely quit the moment we land the job we truly want; but if you omit your Ivy League credentials altogether from these applications, then the large gap in your employment history is presumed due to things such as jail or drugs. Then there's the problem of not having a residential address to offer. Either way, you're perceived as a risk and become stuck in a *damned if you do, damned if you don't* situation.

At the moment, I teach poetry via Zoom to a number of Title I high schools across the country (Title I is a federal program that provides extra funding to help students in high-poverty schools). This pays roughly $1,000 per month, so I receive roughly $4,000 per semester for this. I'd jump at the chance to work full-time at a position such as this, but the hours simply aren't there. I work other jobs, mainly odd jobs, when and where I can. I've authored three books, published countless pieces in reputable and noteworthy journals and magazines, have given guest lectures at community colleges and at Harvard—and the *Veritas* of my situation is that I currently survive on roughly $23,000 per year. That's $23,000 a year that some in my situation would kill for. Many homeless people live on much less than that, but most know the importance of having gratitude for every cent that they *do* have.

I recently had a conversation with a homeless Russian man, a conversation that inspired a poem I included in my next book, *V Verse Is I*. I'll never forget how he reminded me to "always look at the shiny side of the coin, because when we find a coin on the ground, it has its shiny side and its dulled side, so always look for the shiny side." There's a geometry of gratitude in the poetics of homelessness. (I've found a lot of coins since then and always look for the shiny side...)

The last time I saw a raven, I was teaching a class via Zoom on the formal structure of sonnets. It was an orange-vanilla sky morning with a hint of saltwater in the air. I was taking my students for a walk down the train tracks, performatively sharing how the train tracks served as a metaphor for the 14-line limit of the sonnet and how the train symbolized the words of the poem, while the tracks symbolized the structure; expounding how, just as the train would derail if the tracks became warped, the emotional impact of the poem would derail if the structure became warped. We talked about how the "ticket" to attend the sonnet is the attention we pay to it—how we must pay the poem our attention if we're to experience it the way the energy of its structure intends. I concluded the lecture feeling that it had gone well, and as I bent down to put my laptop back in my backpack, I heard a rich, sonorous caw. The raven was perched on the eave of a large, abandoned warehouse a stone's throw away. We locked eyes for a long moment before it swooped down and somersaulted midair, moving away from me. The slant of its movement recalled for me the slant one uses when quoting lines of poetry, "a moment's monument,—/ Memorial from the soul's eternity . . . / its face reveals/ The soul." At that moment, I was *home* with nothing *less* than all I needed.

Desolation Desires

Knock Knock

[To the dead poets who have yet to be born.]

In the Tithing Hall of a place with no proof,
coffinwood papers the sigh our nailing stone—

come in.

Lime Tree

hand, milk, mama,
in that order in
the shape of a Hand—

    a square in the bucket a
    corner in the square
    clang tin a shiny song—

pink cup, coffee, urn,
in that order in
the shape of a House—

clue.

Do something
with the look
of the word—
choose a Flower
Chews a flow-er
from Duncan's
italicized meadow—
there sprouts a ladder
to beauty from the gold
drip of starmelted azure
that hews a legend's maze
Footfall & Rose—a chosen

Often // Eggs

imprint // animal
skull // sleep // tide

    a child's bones bend
    machinery // Jungian

new moon // pipes
27 // horseshoes

    [1 horse only had 3]

tusks // crest
doors // shut(ter)

    in space // slices past
    pyramid // of oftens

Whistles in Tent City

Gideon calls the eskimo
cold in his igloo as polar
bears bash beds to ice in
his mind in throes a hot
thought he ought not a
callous remark but does
& notes with a dimmed
bluebeam Light the fire
that might take his sight
if karma's lacquer forms
too thick to kiss infinity
mirrors into translation

Premonition(s)

An occulting disk, a spiral resurrection
of his wholeness.

A panoply of islands,
such peace in dark water:
it is salt

or asleep, salting.

A greige stone
floats north
of the matrix.

(He) calls to me—
a summer triangle with a star-third joining
Altair above my yellowing staircase.

The Devil Gave Hyla

A well of pumpkin bones
overflows into the hand
of the Ghost of Snow
who topples the flame
that moth's from the wick~

the red prick of a red rose's
thorn, the blue bruise from
the icy rose's burnt thorn—
the poet's pollens in amber
glass, framed on the top of
my tongue—

the nightjar's elegy of dark
earth rings through frantic
worms of July's corn—eye-
ball's a hush-hush of sewn
cherry watervexes—Thoth
& Adam catch their songs.

Night Box a Lace
[alice a nightbox alice]

Ghosts of
past lives
return in
lines and
recall new
meaning.

Two tell me
that I am
what I once
spoke what
one says she
never was.

I adolesce
half-past
them into
a field of
gargantuan
strawberries

& attempt
to rouse a
cold-killed
fire of hail-
hammered
reds whose
dead are fit
to gather

why my only
certainty
here is my
experience of
two perished
permanences.

from The Book of Lines & Borders

carromancy // cry // Jasper speaks
two chambers // of experience glitch

I // circle // back // to // name
the name // I have never // known.

Psycho Some Attics

A decorum of Cordage
tweaks a mirage twicely

chaos is two sandbowls
glued to a quartzing ha-

nd Y raven(ous) Train-
tracks. Nothing makes

sense as it should've ^.
A tilting satellite hinge

Departure

gully an eye lapis
puzzle of begs in
twelve-urn paint
-ings the watery
emeraldine plan-
et of 2 teeth(ing)

The Devil's Mimic of Time

Arrival

Fools: the glare
of the serpents
hillProvidence
breed your sick
pets away from
me: go wrinkle

Order + chaos .•.

Sulfur flicks a bright bite
smokes itself for you.

Settle into the fire, go
tongue-tied then try
speaking for the page
for one day.

On the left,
an orange cone;
on the right
a purple one.

An elephant
in meditative
middle grims
brass—

catch the space
a devil's breath

the one who cleft his foot.

EvillivE

How a void or hole unfilled becomes infilled with evil becomes infiltrated
you're inundated with a masticated black and white *can't be gray* jumping
from blank space to blank space in His name it follows its prey as it hollows
a name for itself after love via *claim* to feel just enough it infills you with shame
borrows your black to snuff out my gray because black only whites and white
only blacks when evil is flipped by the hand of a mirroring thing—
hides in live sight—look, it's a backwarding thing that looks like itself
to feed off my Self to cast me from fishes it casts you a spell *two coins in one well*
tell you shine how you shine when evil goes live it hooks you alive it's the worm
that burrows inside the apple of you to the slant core of truth where half at the core
you are 3 plus 3 more—a geometry of bads—and I an odd window placed sideways
incured above 14 floors that equal the 5 but the truth of the matter only matters on 9 . . .

Do you fragment or salt? Does it matter if marriage? Does a similar marriage
to a hope of some kind? Would a similar marriage divorce absence? It's 6 or
is if I'm watching myself trying to write your name on a mirror with crayon.

gLoss

it's Algood from 10 I See

an inamorata thud, a noble-
less emissary of *nows* pairing

clear as a source of opera-
cry, an oboe ear pinching

a nostalgia, no, mellifluous
sap—the ravens conceived
hatch as gems --magnetic--

in the wind-ascetic physics
of possession in possession

of angels—Θ—a meteoric
temple of sTone windpipes

synthesis rivering catechism

Flip Switch

blood + milk (da ba by)
6 Little Black Birds Tall
A battle scar A day fulla

Demons   who think they
are men—[they never are]

PersonaliT

crystal forest shards
torch the crackback
bloodgame lunatics
when light and dark
switch places in this
place people disapp-
ear/hear—go going
until gone down in
basements or alleys:
they can't have love
so they want power

Absurd the Negatives: Clone

the devil carrot made me do it
the wisdom of afterhours and
how they trade armor [what it
is they midnight know] oh the
crick cold & lethal wax pharao-
nic [reach to touch] as integral
as the consternated flame glass-
ed with fit-filthy odors [of first
things] the aromatic rushing T

cyclical

bloodstream the staircase separate the elements
the name of the math of the chemical wedding
the willing planet of hermaphroditic octahedra
⅓ of a blue sun twitching its story recovering its
chord of music from our hieroglyphic world(s)

continuum

chisel church mice fever
a poet's delirium blood-
rooted—an owl-church
of spinning necks splish
splash the red rope's dye
a ripened grape pastel &
powder—the secret birth
of the painter & the poem

Leonora Takes an Earbone

& tells the past that it belongs to a
monkish man, *a dull knob of a man*
whose voice reminds her of her father
& the page of music she forgot she'd
stuffed inside a hollow figurine she
buried beneath April's Apricot Queen,
some song about patience & brass swans
& a prince's reaction, a song that *sounds
like spoiled fruit looks*, she says, talking
on & on to the past about *particles of
unoriginal air* & how *pain is a tomb
that looms* & why her twice-nightly
dream of *a rude marsh no a rude vision
of a marsh* means she's psychic, a *citrusy*
one not one of those *searing* ones who
escorts those clean-shaven detectives
to some *chocolate nest of bodies some
maze of a bunch of damn bodies*, no,
she has no use for this. She smiles
& sighs, mumbles a question about
crying, why everyone cries as her fingers
discover a small knife—the past tilts
forward & tells her to whittle the
bone into something worth losing.

I was meant for the greenest life, she
reminisces in whimsy, as she carves her
a kiss from the porcelain bit of the man
who went deaf from the hit of a swan &
his daughter's "Good God!" green music.

Rose of Jericho

theory of a cure: black rainbow:

Doctor, I have applied my full
attention to your grave . . .

A rosary rinsed
in a grape antique
click of a crab-lock—

fortune favors all things
as accidents.

An oaken cage assembled in threes
from quickbeam—sporadic knob-
conjectures of an evil mind, static:

# Eudemonic Possession

Yellow Requited

mouthfuls of aster-
isms under a baby-
blue sky, stay, Hi—
sway-say jonquil
the elephantine
blond with his
linden-heart's
four-chambered
lemon: long gone?

He (Exist)

An afterimage
sits on the intellectual seat
of my heart—

a continuum of
personhoods
in full spectrum—

each color a specter
the flints of his name
unfacing my once-face   in danger—

Itty Bitty

a giant's grace
as full as
a giant's reality

A True Dimension of Nothingness

A motion of smoke.
A burn-blue apple.
An interior
cause of things.

A deep
authentic bite.
A satisfactory
tooth of a core.

Fire coming upon
such a world—

From such things
will make a test—

An obitual soot.
A sprain of work.
A reactionary
pulp of searing things.

Lucky

In a starling's mud

irradiated eyes
feed my "am"s

(carnal cadences
of estrangement)

fissured & wine-
colored, staind &

orphaned & un-
named the same—

Isle of Eeries

cut by their symbols a linguistics of Litter thrashed
about The Day of Unknowns, blame the Frog that
kept his tail—{fit for sacred Rage}—{ages that age}

Idealization X

The subject of the stone remains deep on the bone of experience:

finders
keepers
the keymaker's
reaper as radiant
as a rose disrobing.

Pete (False, Oh)

clip clop ovAlly shoe
cry The noose Loose

Yellow Unrequited

psychoses of heart
the fruit of joined
life worked high—
a soft jacket habit
jackrabbit's habit
silenced rabid—
lover: What ends
when our simile is
replaced by the act?

Exi(s)ting the Mirror

Hushing V

Somewhere the bad geese are laughing
and by laughing I mean incredulously
I mean wouldn't it sound nonetheless
as if a time spent unstuck in lull-speck-
ed hush shouldn't be spent on a letter
an open letter to better a circumstance
under no *I*'s control—and who knows
who's in control as showers turn snow
on the edge of a gray volant echelon V,
my dam-aged morrow-tuned eye acute
[we're a quivering goose a good geese].

I don't know, maybe the thing
[I don't know anything except]
I know what I don't yet believe.
[I know what I do believe I do]
I know *I* could go, and that's a
thing worth considering funny.

An Our Wasp

Stone tips forward onto stone
in the tone of Crispin's plums
sleepers black walnuts & night-
shade a requiem kingdom-sail
& Adam's song a woolen harm-
onium of shellholes fires brick
back to mud [verso] i.e. finger-
foliums of sleek grass sugaring
Horn of Amalthea [recto] as I
tie a triangle of nerves nervous.

A Thing Too Much of Not

How is it the French woman
asks but I do not know why
she asks me how it is because
I don't even know what it is
[it's a concatenation of an age,
a wettened and odd-oiled thing]
yet she knows I rely on the word
thing too much; however, isn't
it poetry that relies on the word
too much, or: what if the word
isn't used by the poet nearly
enough? I mean, let's look
at some synonyms for *thing*:
we have, well, okay—I do
like *instrument*, though now
my [in]body centers on harmony
& melody, not the savory *thing*,
& while I see *object* as a healthy
pick, it feels safe, overcooked
[a chunk of sharp meat sans fat,
figures]. Oh, remand me to erase
the word *remand*, as it stirs up
re-*mind* . . . when you're done
with me let me know & I'll go.

4 1 4 4

I fetch fox's fireburn
4 from 13 caves hid
by the sun's 6 clocks:
"Look"— I Look —

a ouija'd 4-shark'd
sin-timed pleasure
cone of cures on 1
thin basilica growl.

Trip Tick Talk

A normative depository
of divine revelation
in a theater of maligned
abnegation afterwashed
in the sin of refusing
to acknowledge one's
knowledge: to have a god
one can control is to have
a god [who controls the haver].

Does aseity belong
only to those with
sight? By definition
a creature owes
its existence
to its creator—
so it is written.
[I am an alone fountain
on an unhesitating ascent.]

Us, anonymous feathers,
remain glued to the sludge
of a scheme on our beam
of brokedown things,
of vitreous vertigos—[I]

enter the dwelling place
of dead tenderness alive
where rats with big legs
& ballerina eyes surmise—

The Unknowing Cloud Oned With

You and I multiply and I return to the dream
divining our coffee grounds at the bottom
of a lake of sunken scales [laking]—a quick-
ening at the base:

rootquake
mandrake
simulacra
concinnate
lacuna
nival [hecatomb]
secreted [teardrops]
lintel & fiddleheads
the silver cord of full shadow

curls under the stone of this poem as if
a tender suffix or a salamander jeweling.

I at the Source

I uses a large bundle of twigs
to set some lakeside trees on fire.
I is on the shore of an original place.
I recites something that I am not allowed to remember as *I* lights the thin trees on fire.
I is not who I am when I am awake, no, *I* is a sentience a sentence of difference in making.
Flames begin to roll while the whole of me who is watching *I* light the trees on fire realizes th
I is the thinker thinking the fire into first thought—the pinkening orange hue my first horizo
I is two and "I" is, too.
I simultaneously holds the torch while observing the one who holds the torch.
I witness *I* create the colors of my first horizon.
I is an oldest sense a first ancestor a fire within and without.
I is both the creator and the created.
~ ens increatum et ens creatum ~
V is My
I is *I*

Encountered [To the Poet in the Stone Wall]

The stone wall [poetry] knows how the I and You
multiply, how the otherness between the two
contains multitudes, and how, if we're
not careful, one will
consume the other,
leaving only
I—

◐ On Poetry ◑

Encounter

The poetic concept of encounter
dictates that to live a poetically-
charged existence, one must
demand from life a mosaic
of dynamic human and non-
human encounters,
writing through the ghosts
of the things one's meant
to befriend to collectively
forge the agreement with death
that life requires, measured
on a scale of joy and suffering
by the weight of one's participation
in the truth of things; therefore, I—

Poems are sleeping things. Poems are experiences of encounters that fall fast asleep in poetry's arms to the music of a poet's language. A reader of poetry—an *addressee*—works to awaken the poem so that it can in turn awaken something within them. We awaken poems to awaken something within ourselves. To awaken a poem, we pay the poem our attention. Attention is the ticket to *attend* a poem, and we attend a poem much as we would any event, with the intention of experiencing a thing worth experiencing.

Poetry acquires
        then causes
                the mind

to unlock the door lock the door more
to unlock the door lock the door more
to unlock the door lock the door more

some thing is othering
some other thing more

Poetry is older than language itself; it was nameless until language was born and only then did it become, as we know it today, *literary art*. Poetry was born from repetition—planetary orbits, sunrise/sunset, full and new/waxing and waning moons, the ebb and flow of the ocean's tide, etc.—the friction caused by poetry coming into contact with itself via symbol via language via intellect and creative energy causes meaning to spark forth new intention, what we call *metaphor*, which contains the pure energy-seed of poetry and language's closest living relative to the original noninflectional language of symbol. When poetry was new to language, and as children do, it used repetition to praise, learn, transform and persevere: "I think I can, I think I can, I think I can . . . "—and it still does.

"Poetry"

the poems do
not belong to
the poet: this
poetry knows

In poetry, desolation desires to empty the memory of itself. Poetry exists to help us navigate the deep dark rivers of self and the collective by creating this illuminating our beneaths (beliefs) with the light of imagination and promise and the possibility of what could in isolation be found in desolation, or in the desolation of faith, where observation and participation lead to imagination and promise.

Desolation desires to empty the memory of itself because it knows that it only exists when something has left it. (How us poets only feel we truly exist when something has left us, when the poem of the moment is completed then released.) No one, no thing, nothing, desires to be left in the darkness of unfulfilled desire. Does darkness? Memory exposes Light even if the memory is dark.

Poetry is the desire of itself fulfilled. It is desire-full, thus desirable. It is memory-full, thus memorable. Poetry still exists in a world that no longer monetarily rewards it because memory still exists in this world. Where there is memory, there is poetry. (Erase the mind, erase the line.)

◐ On Madness ◑

And I have found both freedom and safety in my madness; the freedom of loneliness and the safety from being understood, for those who understand us enslave something in us.

But let me not be too proud of my safety. Even a Thief in a jail is safe from another thief.

—Khalil Gibran

I must preface the preceding essay by confessing that I knew next to nothing about what I was actually addressing at the time, for my intellect and creative energy were engrossed in a very real and very spiritual hell that, in turn, spawned these "realizations" and writings. At the time, while in physical and psychological turmoil, while experiencing my at-some-point-every-artist-goes-mad madness—which, funny enough, came after my book *A Madness of Blue Obsidian* was released—I'd thought, in a way, that I'd unlocked some mysteries of good and evil and that I was doing good work in writing it out of my body and mind, but little did I know that I was writing from an evil body and mind.

I was being hit with an innumerable amount of *Satan's fiery darts*, so they say, so much so that my perpetually being in the wrong places at the wrong times with the wrong (wicked) people drove me into a state of, well, sheer madness. I was sleeping very little while becoming utterly obsessed with personality disorders, hungrily needing to know why some people were the way they were, why they were, for lack of a better word but nonetheless true, evil (in my case). In a very intense space of two years, my life became black and white, a mirroring thing, of sorts, with my intellect ever-stretching to mirror the thought-processes of the many dangerously untreated Cluster B personalities and dichotomous thinkers I was attracting into my daily experience at a mind-bending rate.

This experience stemmed from falling in love with someone who suffered from a severely untreated case of what some call Borderline Personality Disorder, though I no longer agree with this label or notion, as I've learned that these complex *humannesses*, such as intense emotional turbulence and deep insecurity stemming from horrific childhood traumas, are too complex and fragile, dangerous even, to label; however, from my dynamically deep personal experiences with antisocial personalities, I'm now convinced that the once love of my life was not "mentally ill" but rather possessed by, well, demons. I had to nearly lose my life multiple times by the hands of this soulmate and accompanying "flying monkeys" to realize that demons *are* people, to realize the *reality* and *inevitability* of how true evil can and does manifest itself in people, in *real* "everyday" people (thinking of Martha Stout's *The Sociopath Next Door* here). This is all to say: When people have *real* demons, they are demonic. Period. (Matthew 12:43-45). And I use the term *soulmate* here because although this relationship was highly toxic and nearly drove me mad with the gaslighting and such, looking back now, I know that it was purposed to be. God allowed me to experience the intense levels of pain and grief I experienced so that I would someday see what type of sinful life I myself was living, to see, despite my firm beliefs in spiritualism and animism for so long, that I was in fact a Christian, or at least now called to be. God was the only one who could've saved my physical and spiritual, and emotional, life during this time, and He did.

I, like you, am no angel. I realize my own shortcomings as a person, and particularly as a person who was once in a toxic trauma-bonded relationship. I was very much what some would call a codependent caretaker, which stems from my own insecurities of not feeling worthy of love and trust and loyalty. Again, it's a mirroring thing. Everyone is our mirror. I discovered a lot about myself while in relationship with these personalities. I was and am no better than anybody else. This I know. I hope that this shows in my work here, for in it, part of me perpetually grieves.

I should be dead today, by either another's hand or mine, but I'm alive because of Him. I was caught in some wicked snares, some complex confusions and deep griefs and the whole mess of evil things, and the poet in me had nowhere to go but to the page after having dove deeper and deeper into minds, both others and my own, that were becoming more and more skewed by darkness. I thought I was discovering things. I thought I was curing things. But, I was simply . . . mad . . . in every definition of the word. What makes a poet a true seer of things if they can't themselves see when they've gone mad? I lost everything, including nearly my mind for good, but I would not change a thing. I'm grateful for all of it. I'm grateful for every demon I had to battle, including my own. My only regret is that I couldn't save the one I loved from theirs. I learned this hard lesson in the most utterly heartbreaking, and terrifying, way.

Many of the poems in this book were written while in my Hell. Many are coded abstract, not due to my usual poetic inclinations and motivations tied to Surrealism and Modernism, but because there is still no true clarity for me. Many of the poems that share this book with the following essay *are* confusing because experiences of real evil are utterly confusing. Evil confuses and confounds, it makes us question, it hijacks our intuitions and steals our light. I try my best here to translate this personal confusion via poetry.

That all written, I wrote the following essay on April 8, 2024, during a total solar eclipse and, fittingly enough, at the height of my being in the depths of Hell, and it's important to note that this declarative *Let There Be Evil* essay—along with nearly all else written in this book and written pre-*Nova Qua Nova*—was written before I was saved by Christ. For this reason, I cannot bring myself to return to this essay to perform the necessary edits it likely requires to guarantee smoother reading. I nearly deleted this essay altogether, but doing so would dishonor the moments in my thinking life that served as intellectual keystones to my eventual soul's salvation, so this draft of a telling essay must stay, even if I cannot return to it myself. I leave below, in all its disorderliness and repetitive chaos, with the hope that something in it can offer something of value to someone, somewhere.

Let There Be Evil: Holy Darkness and the Problem with Our Perception of "Light"

"O maker of proud planet's negative,
obscure the scalding sun till no clocks move."
—Sylvia Plath, "Sonnet to Satan"

If 1,000,000 people simultaneously stood at the edge of a dense forest at 2:00 PM, with the sun high and the sky azure-pure save for one or three opulent clouds, and if those 1,000,000 people were tasked with having to get through the dense forest on foot on a mark-get-set-go, what would happen? As with any group of people, they would likely feel as if they were in a race, and most would begin moving quickly through the dense forest until they undoubtedly reached some sort of clear and definitive finishing line. Under the light of the sun, the collective task of the species quickly becomes a competition to see who will ultimately win and who will ultimately lose.

Let's suppose, though, that if after those 1,000,000 people set foot into that dense forest the sun all of a sudden went dark, or totally eclipsed; what would happen? Those 1,000,000 people would now be in a pitch-black dense forest with no light to help guide their way, and they would no longer be participating in a race rather an individual journey through unseen, unknown, thus feared territory, relegated to having to rely on their other senses, including intuition, to help guide them to safety; however, what if one out of the 1,000,000 people were blind, or had previously experienced having to traverse alone through a similar dense forest in the dark?

This one person would already know that the key to making it through the forest is to take things slowly with the aim of learning and knowing their surroundings. This person would be psychologically skilled enough to face any underlying fears that the Darkness of the forest would bring, and this person would already know the reward that comes with facing a fear of the unknown—becoming stronger, more resilient, reliable, and essentially, more whole a person, or perhaps more *Holy*, if we look at the etymology of that word. With 999,999 people suddenly stopped in their tracks, only the one who has already walked the path of Darkness would know that the Darkness brings relief to the eyes, unlike Light, which can make one go blind if they were to stare into its brilliance for too long. One who has already traversed Darkness knows what Darkness hides—nothing that is not also present in Light—and having already carefully traversed the inner and outer landscapes of Darkness, this person knows that with a step, they could trip over a stone or walk carelessly over a cliff's edge, because being in Darkness before required them to slow down and become acquainted with their immediate surroundings. Darkness teaches us that trusting in oneself is a must and that when we traverse Darkness, we need only trust two things: our intuitions, and the knowledge that our body—coupled with the will to move our feet—will move us toward where we need to go and, ultimately, to who we must become.

When in Light, when trusting *only* in Light's ability to guide, people are like sheep—suitably, biblical sheep—meandering mindlessly along as one of the herd who, with blind faith, trust that their shepherd is keeping them safe—trusting outwardly but not inwardly. When in Darkness, when trusting *only* in one's senses and intuition, people are like goats—suitably, biblical scapegoats—outcasted to their deserts of self-reliance made to survive by sheer instinct and intuition.

We know that if one experiences too much Light, one becomes blind or sunburnt, often quite quickly; we also know that if one experiences too much Darkness, one becomes cold or confused, often quite slowly. Light can blind just as night can bind.

Light guides us outwardly and can show us to safety and when to rest. Darkness guides us inwardly, asking us to rely on our instincts and intuitions rather than external forces, and it can show us what we fear and when to either run toward or away from something. Light can keep us still to the point of stagnancy, while Darkness can keep us moving to the point of exhaustion, if we move through Darkness with the sole intent of making it to Light as quickly as possible, which is when Darkness becomes Evil, instilling fear instead of the motivation to learn how to overcome fear.

A pond, say a typical idyllic pond in the country, can seem harmless, peaceful, and inviting. A quick-moving river on a mountain or in a canyon, say a whitewater rapid, can seem dangerous, chaotic, and repellent; however, the idyllic country pond, often cloaked in that beautiful green algae, is toxic. The pond water stays still and becomes stagnant, and becomes home to a host of deadly bacteria, viruses, parasites, leeches, and so on. We know that if we were to go swimming in this pond or even swallow only a few drops of its water, we could become sick or violently ill to the point of death. To take refuge in stagnancy makes us stagnant. The whitewater rapid, on the other hand, remains clear and pristine in its purity. It is strong enough to cleanse itself and us, and can even carve new paths for itself out of bedrock or clay, and sometimes, its water is not only safe for us to drink but incredibly beneficial. Even the notions of *safety* and *danger* both contain within them their Good or Evil counterpart, and it is not that a thing is ever truly safe or dangerous, it is only our respect for that thing, or lack of respect for that thing, that determines its level of safety or danger for us. Ponds are both safe and dangerous. Whitewater rapids are both safe and dangerous. Everything, every *thing*, contains duality; if it does not, then it is nothing, no *thing*, and whatever the no-thing may be wouldn't matter because it simply wouldn't and doesn't exist. *Nothing* cannot exist without *something*, unless it is the only thing in existence that has no counterpart, which happens to be the only thing outside our capacity for comprehending existence—the cosmic void of space, the only pure void in known existence, pure Darkness.

Death is an agreement with life that death exists and life is an agreement with death that life exists, and to reiterate, one thing, such as life, cannot exist without its counterpart, death—both elements are of the one thing and are merely situated in a different place on the same spectrum, existence—and as the Hermetic philosophy of *as above, so below, as within, so without* dictates (compare The Emerald Tablets with Moses' Ten Commandments Tablets)—we cannot be or have one of a thing without also having or being that thing's counterpart. Here, we have the dilemma of *otherness* and *being*. While we are *being*, we are also experiencing *otherness*, and if we consider that *otherness* is Light—the totality of the color spectrum—then *being* must be the opposite of the totality of the color spectrum, or the opposite of all color itself, which is black, or the pure being-ness of Darkness.

Everything contains Light and Darkness. Everything is Good and Evil. Duality indeed states that a thing cannot exist without that one thing's counterpart. We are taught that in the beginning, God created the heaven and the earth; however, if we consider God as the original thinker who came to manifest humankind through His Word, then it could be said that God, the original thinker, was a hermaphrodite—let us recall Hermes from Thoth, Hermetic philosophy, and *hermetically sealed* here—the original *every thing* rolled into one—which, when deconstructed, is essentially Baphomet, the Western esoteric and occult symbol of Darkness and Evil. God could not have created heaven without creating the earth because one could not have existed without the other, just as hot could not exist without cold, how wetness could not exist without dryness, and if we replace the word *earth* there with the word *Hell*, then we now have a perfectly logical duality that complements the collective notion of *Hell on earth*; therefore, humans are, as the law of duality dictates, both Good and Evil, divine and wicked. Our free will—notwithstanding the duality of *fate* and *destiny*—only comes into play at the end of our lives, when, after having lived an existence of both Good and Evil, are asked to answer the one question we are each here to answer: "Now that you've lived both, which do you choose: do you choose Good, or do you choose Evil?"

It's important to note that even the Bible itself is both Good and Evil if we consider that the total number of books in today's standard Bible is 66—which equals the number 3 in numerology, an Evil number since it cannot be divided equally—while there is a second "total number of books in the Bible," 73—the number of which equals the number 1 in numerology, the original number of the original thinker-hermaphrodite, Baphomet. Even the Bible, how it's read and perceived today, contains both Good *and* Evil elements. That written, I must recall Isaiah 5:20, which states: "Woe unto them that call evil good, and good evil; that put darkness for light, and light for darkness; that put bitter for sweet, and sweet for bitter!" In writing this essay, I perceive this in two ways, and both ways are correct.

Scripture tells us that God created Light and divided it from Darkness, which means Darkness was the original form and still is if we view original Darkness as *the* void from which all came forth. We look to the night sky knowing that if it weren't for our sun, which we know will eventually burn out, we would be in perpetual Darkness. Darkness always was, is, and will be, while Light was created after and within Darkness and will eventually cease to exist, if we consider black holes the eventual end of the universe as we perceive or know it. Light divides Darkness as it moves through space, which makes Light a perpetually moving thief. To be Light, Light requires every known color to collectively simultaneously exist. Light only exists by stealing every possible element of the larger thing it needs to exist—color. Black, or pure cosmic Darkness, requires nothing to exist for it *is* nothing, it is *no thing*, and since it is *no thing*, then no other thing can fully know it let alone steal it, thus Light had to be created from within Darkness to offset the nothingness of Darkness and balance it out for creation, for creatures, to exist. If Baphomet is our true perception of Evil and constitutes our negative beliefs about Darkness, then why did God need to create a color spectrum within Darkness to then steal from Darkness to create Light to "divide" Darkness into two? This means that God cut the energy of Baphomet in half to create duality, man and woman, etc., and wouldn't this mean that God, or our perception of God, is also Evil? After all, God cannot exist with Baphomet, or Satan, for if He could, what would He be? He would be Baphomet, the original hermaphroditic *creature* that some would consider perfect in form and symbolism. God and Baphomet (or Satan) both contain Light and Darkness and are of Light and Darkness. Darkness became *Holy Darkness* once Light was born with the mission to divide Darkness into two, but when working together in balance, they can both be good and create new things such as math, life, creatures, etc.

By definition, a *creature* owes its existence to another, a creator, for only a creator can create a creature that is also able to create. Where did the first creator originate? The original creator was itself a creature but since it existed before anything it created, duality did not yet exist, therefore the original creator was both male and female, both animal and man, Good and Evil. Baphomet, a deified creature, embodies these traits and is the ultimate symbol of balance, and, etymologically, his name recalls the first prophet, Muhammed, if we consider that Baphomet, or Mahomet, is simply the bastardized version of the name Muhammed.

As humans with souls and free will—notwithstanding the duality of *fate* and *destiny*—we are tasked to view ourselves as the mirrors of our maker, and when we experience ourselves being mirrored back to ourselves through the perceptions thus reactions of others—which, as with everything, can be Good or Evil; the Evil example being the dark psychological mirroring that occurs when speaking or relating with an untreated Cluster B personality-type such as a psychopath, sociopath, narcissist, Machiavellian, etc.—we come to realize that we are not so much creations of God as we are recreations of a god-animal, as we ourselves are both god-like and animal-like. We are not necessarily humankind made in God's image rather simply an image that exists on both sides of itself, and like the coin found face-up in the dirt that we are all born as (sinners), we each have a shiny side and a dirty side. Some people are angels and some people are demons. All people are Good and Evil, some are just more one than the other. The problem is that our perceptions of Light have made us blind to the real Evil that exists in our world on an everyday person-to-person relational level.

There are an estimated 8.1 billion people on this planet, which means that there are 8.1 billion different realities, and as people, we each move through this world on the ledge of experience, overlooking proverbial water and fire, joy and suffering, as we capture glimpses of our rippling selves therein and thereafter—individual reality is nothing but a continuum of personhoods in spiritual and creative pursuit—and the deficit of every person on this planet is that every person will spend their lifetime having to learn how to relate to every other person who is not them. These relations, or relational interactions, at their core, conjure either the Light or Darkness within us, Good or Evil. And as it goes, everyone is our mirror. Think about the energy you feel when relating to another. At the end of any interaction, you are left feeling either better or worse than before—and do not let the illusion of neutrality fool you; there is no true neutrality possible in any person-to-person interaction, for neutrality, or feeling neutral about an interaction, is merely a blip in acceptance, a form of denial centered somewhere slightly above the feeling of being either accepted or being rejected by another accepting or rejecting person. At the conclusion of any person-to-person interaction, you experience either a lightening or darkening of your energy; whether you peer that deeply into your feelings to recognize this is on you, but I assert that this is true.

As a poet, I'd be remiss to not share a short poem I wrote about a conversation I once had with a homeless Russian man who, while standing outside his church in the rain one late night in Harvard Square, shared a cigarette with me while teaching me the importance of looking at life as if it were the "shiny side of the coin we find face-up in the dirt," hence my aforementioned metaphor on us having our shiny and dirty sides:

A homeless Russian man tells me
that I should always only envision
the shiny side of the coin—

found face up. We are smoking
in front of his church in the rain.

Just like the coin, we all have a Light side and a Dark side, living both righteously and wickedly as we traverse life, in these bodies on this planet at this time, until we arrive spirit-to-spirit with our creator, prepared to answer that one aforementioned question of which side do we choose.

When we are born into this world, the first thing we do is inhale a deep breath, and then we cry. The last thing we'll do in this world is exhale a deep breath, and then others will cry for us. We breathe duality.

Most of us have become engrained with the belief that Light is Good, divine, Holy, and healing, and that Darkness is Evil, profane, wicked, and to be feared. We are taught that the "color" black—which isn't a color at all rather the absence of all color—means putrefaction and decomposition, the "color" of a burning thing burnt. In alchemy, *nigredo* or *blackness* refers to the original substances—material and spiritual—that must be cleansed and cooked in the first step on the path toward creating the Philosopher's Stone. That written, and for the aim of this essay, let's mirror this belief for a moment and perceive Light as Evil and Darkness as Good. Good and Evil are in everything, including language. The English word for *evil*, when mirrored, is *live*. When we mirror the saying back to ourselves, we are told to *live evil*. Does the mirroring tell us that we should live demonically? No. The mirroring of the duality simply tells us that there is a second meaning to the word *evil* that we have forgotten—we are being told that *evil* is also Good, because even our perceptions are dual; we cannot be told to live a life of Evil without also being told to live a life of Good. Life is not inherently Good. Life is not inherently Evil. Life is inherently both thus language is inherently both. Consider the goodness that language gifts to us while also considering the confusion and chaos it creates for us. Duality contains a cyclical element, which I won't go into here, but we must also consider how symbol is the original and only non-inflectional language, and when we compare the ancient use of pictographs and hieroglyphs to the modern use of emojis (or *glyphs*), this too is evidence of the Good and Evil in language, as symbols, pictographs, and hieroglyphs contain and embody a timeless beauty and humanness that emojis or digital glyphs cannot. The word *hieroglyph* means "sacred carving" or "the god's words." *Hiero* means "sacred," while the word *glyph* means "a small graphic symbol." We have literally replaced sacredness with something *graphic*, which, aside from being defined as something related to a visual or artistic work, also denotes something as shocking or vivid that gives a clear visual impression in words, the keyword being *impression*. *Time* is another thing that also gives us the impression of something that is not always natural, or even real.

We know that time is a construct that humankind has created for itself which means that time is also Good and Evil. When we do Good things for ourselves, such as when we meditate, when we feel sustained peace or ecstatic joy or love, or anytime we feel a familiar emotion at a new positive intensity, in these moments, time often feels as if it has slowed or even stopped. Why is this? Well, we slow or stop time when we slow or stop our minds—we *mind* time and time *minds* us. When we do Evil things to ourselves, time speeds up and catapults us forward, but not in positive ways. When a person uses certain substances such as caffeine, nicotine, cocaine, or amphetamines, time can become accelerated to the point of forgoing sleep or food for two or more days straight, essentially tricking the person into feeling as if only a handful of hours have gone by, and this tricking of time—the devil's mimic of time, I like to call it—due to consuming things that are toxic to us, is the Evil side of time. Time, when Evil, rapidly ages us by stealing our Darkness, for if time's Evil side steals our sleep, dreams, meditations, and our health, things that are only attainable to us when we are asleep or sleep properly, in our inward Darknesses, then this is Evil time stealing our Holy Darkness. Time heals and steals.

Having touched on space and time, it's important to note that the term and notion of *space and time* is a pertinent example of what we assume go together but don't: space is Darkness and if the cosmic void of space is the original *something*, then time cannot be its counterpart in duality because humans made time, but humans did not make space. If we replace the word time and the notion thereof with the word math, with the notion of universal math, which, like space, existed before us and will exist after us—while knowing that time is not math and that is does not, for example, contain the golden ratio, the Fibonacci Sequence—then the correct term, the one that contains proper duality, is *space and math*. Furthermore, if we look at this mathematically with the knowledge that Darkness is the original first *thing* and does not move and is, therefore, the number 0, which makes mathematics the second *thing* that does move and is, therefore, the number 1—the first movement of creation that moves away from 0 to become 1—and if we marry the two things together into their one original number, we arrive at the hermaphroditic number 1 and the base ingredients of creation and thus duality itself—space and math constitute Darkness and are both the same thing. Space and math cannot truly be combined because 0 plus 1 equals only the one, and it (space and math as one thing) equals 1 and not 2 because space and math *are* the original creator, the original hermaphroditic energy of creation, or Baphomet. (I use Baphomet as an example throughout this essay to show how we are often swayed from seeking the truth in places that are collectively believed to be Evil. And the more we see a thing and learn about it, the more desensitized we become to it. I believe we must fully know all the Good and Evil we can if we are to ever truly fully know ourselves.)

Time is not natural, it is Evil Light in disguise. We know how time can be Good, but like everything, it is also Evil, particularly when it sucks the life-blood from the body to which it itself belongs—Evil time can be a tick stuck to our bodies, taking and taking while leaving only a small pain yet much larger unforeseen disease in the making; it can be an Evil clock tick-ing, ticking some distorted sound for no rhyme or reason that only leaves us deaf to sound reasoning. In absolute Darkness, there is no time, and in Light, there is only time. This is evident in how Light moves through Darkness and in the existence of lightyears. Darkness only *is* and is perpetually present in the now, it is outside of time, while Light only moves through Darkness, creating time; however, for life to exist at all, Darkness needs Light and vice versa, and here we have a perfect example of the perfect balance needed to create something as miraculous and brilliant as life. That written, our perceptions are mirrored: the reality is that Darkness contains the real Holy divinity that we're taught only resides in Light because Darkness exists with or without Light while Light can only exist in Darkness. Light divides Darkness and can do so in Good and Evil ways.

Thinking of *the devil's mimic of time* and the metaphoric tick of its disease, let's look at disease, or dis-ease. We know that a cancerous tumor can only exist in a living body while a living body can only exist healthily without a cancerous tumor. A cancerous tumor is Evil to us, a well-perceived Evil, but we need Light (radiation) to destroy the tumor, and this is where Light is Good. Too much Light, though, and the whole body burns, as Light can only crack Darkness open so much until Light becomes Evil, or destructive. Light, like Darkness, has the power to both create and destroy purities. With radiation, Light divides the Evil Darkness of the tumor by damaging its DNA to the point of annihilation. Holy Darkness, however, *allows* itself to crack open for Light because it knows that it does not need Good or Evil Light to exist but that *life* needs Good Light to exist.

You and I are nothing but moths to a flame, born with an impossible propensity for self-destruction once dominant Light appears in our dark periphery. Holy Darkness witnesses us make the perpetual mistake of turning our intellectual and spiritual backs to Darkness while believing that Light is the only and ultimate Good, but Holy Darkness knows that Light can deceive just as Darkness can deceive, and as a species, is it not true that we are deceived so easily, and often purposely? As both Thomas Aquinas and C.S. Lewis teach, for Evil to succeed, Evil must disguise itself as Good—the moth believes that going into the flame is Good—and if we continue to unknowingly cling steadfastly to this misbelief, our distorted notions of Light and Darkness will continue to arrest our understanding of things and self until we are nothing but prisoners of our reactions to life and others. Our misbelief in Darkness does good work in enticing and luring us toward spiritual death. We are moths, continuing to believe only in Good Light while ignoring the Evil it also contains, and as moths do, we continue to flicker insatiably toward and around a misbelief that is controlled by truly maleficent energies—human and non-human—whose unappeasable desire to deceptively steal our Good Light is exponentially greater than our desire to open our eyes to Holy Darkness and live it.

"For in much wisdom is much grief: and he that increaseth knowledge increaseth sorrow."

(Ecclesiastes 1:18)

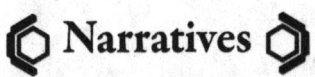

Narratives

A New Fire

It's Saturday night and I've been working since 10 AM. It's been years since I've had a Saturday night off, but I like this job, and when I'm lucky, it pays the rent. The bars are letting out and I get a call from my boss: "Jason, can you head to Main Street and pick up my brother? He's drunk and I'm stuck with the kids and don't want him driving. He's wearing a black suit and will be outside. I'll throw you $30 for the trouble." "Sure thing." "Shukran."

He gets in the back of the cab reeking of hookah and alcohol, but I like the smell, and luckily he is a happy drunk. He asks me how long I've been driving a taxi and how long I've worked for his brother. "Eight years." He leans forward, puts his hand on my shoulder and casually says, in a thick Arabic accent, "You will have a hard life. If this is where you are right now, you're going to have a hard rest of your life." He removes his hand from my shoulder and slumps back into his seat. I crack my window and light a cigarette. "You can smoke in here?" he asks, enthusiastically. "No."

It's Sunday and the sun is rising. Heading home for my usual intermittent nap, I pull onto the on-ramp and notice a trail of black smoke rising from the chimney of a crematory in an adjacent cemetery. I wonder if it is a body being burned, if the smoke has a name, and I wonder if living a hard life means dying a hard death. It is snowing.

In burnt-ivory morning air, an ensouled plume inks the sky from the chimney of a stone crematory on a hill in the woods.

I think of the line of poetry that the smoke inspires and begin thinking about how poetry first made its way into my life, about Khalil Gibran, and about how he wrote to the madman while being supported by a wealthy patroness in some literary city, Boston or New York, I think. I remember first reading *The Prophet* at 17 and falling in love with the idea that one could endure poverty if they believed it forged the one

105

true path to God. I don't know about God, but I know about god, about poetry and her muse, and about how it feels to create something of an energy that can never be destroyed, or taken away from me, though my father occasionally tries.

A crow once told me, one afternoon while I was sitting in the taxi at the beach waiting for a call, that I was a poet. I didn't believe him, but he reminded me of my grandfather, the way he bent backward as he walked, and his caw was insistent. Ever since I was a child, I always did perceive myself in two worlds. I still remember my imaginary friends from when I was a kid, the ones that lived in what I called "tree caves." One was named Gotzameel. He was short, dressed in all black, and wore a big round hat. Imaginary or not, he was a real friend. A couple of years later, around the age of 5, I told my mother a story about how in my mind I saw a stone in a wall fall and split open and spill milk everywhere. She said I used the term "mother's milk" and that it freaked her out a bit. In daydream, I often think of Gotzameel, the tree caves, and that stone. I think of the milkstone and ponder if the stones that make-up the walls of the crematory on the hill in the woods contain milk.

A crematory contains two burning-chambers fueled by natural gas. If you see black smoke emitting from a crematory's chimney, this indicates that one of the chambers is overheated due to an incomplete combustion. Any noticeable odors or visible smoke is due to an incomplete combustion. Incomplete combustion occurs when there is an inadequate supply of air or oxygen.

"Hey, your brother called. He wants to know if you can stop by the jail and put $50 in his canteen. He says he needs socks and candy bars. I know. I'm sorry."

My mother has been working at Wal-Mart for seven years. She was hired as a full-time employee and recently hit her pay cap. The company is now demoting all full-time capped employees to part time and cutting their benefits, so answering my brother's collect call from jail is the most she can do. Standing in one spot at a cash register day-in-day-out for years has ruined her knees and she now needs a total replacement, which she will get once her SSDI application gets approved. A total knee replacement requires a significant cutting away of damaged cartilage and bone. The heart-shaped kneecap, the patella, is removed then replaced with a prosthesis. Artificial joints are used to secure the prosthesis to the ends of the femur and tibia, ends which are replaced by metal. Once both ends are secured, the knee is flexed then stitched. My mother has traded two heart-shaped bones and thousands of hours of her life to make ends meet.

It takes 2-3 hours to cremate a body. During this time, all but the bones are incinerated. Once the cremation chamber cools, the bones are removed from the retort and pulverized. When someone is given the ashes of a loved one, they are not given ashes, they are given pulverized bone.

Once a fragile container of memories to come, now an obsidian crest to the knowable world—a lumpy, decanted moment—how time appears as change appears.

My brother, a repeat offender, was convicted of drug-trafficking charges and sentenced to 7 years in state prison. Though he has up to this point been in and out of prison for 15 years, this will be his longest stint yet. Detectives raided his place after a year-long investigation, shortly after he had successfully escaped two high-speed pursuits through town. We are a year-and-a-half apart in age but have never been close. As we grew older, our relationship became measured by how many lines of coke were left on the plate. He was one of the biggest drug dealers south of Boston. He never worried much about getting caught because prison no longer scared him, he had become desensitized to it. He also had enough money to keep the best lawyer on retainer, a lawyer who is able to reduce a mandatory 25-year sentence down to 7 because he golfs with the judge. A week after the police raided his place, I read in the paper that they had seized 116 grams of cocaine with a street value of $20,000, 4 grams of fentanyl, and $5,000 in cash. The last time I was at his place, I watched him get into an argument with his pregnant girlfriend and point a loaded gun at her head. I grabbed her arm and rushed her outside and into my car, drove her to her mother's house and gave her some money for shoes, since she didn't have time to grab her shoes. Before they began arguing, I noticed that his mattress was peppered with numerous black holes and that the carpet directly below was covered in ash. This meant that my brother had begun using. The burn holes were from cigarettes he had lit then accidentally dropped after sticking a needle into his arm and passing out. "Monkeys can't sell bananas," he would always say, but he was never good at taking advice, even if it was his own. How his mattress never fully caught on fire is still a mystery to me. An incomplete combustion.

The temperature of the furnace must remain between 1600-1800 degrees. Harmful emissions are a byproduct of incomplete combustion and are produced by the fire in the primary chamber during the consumption of the body. Black smoke, ash, or soot indicates an incomplete combustion.

My phone rings. Unknown number. It's my father. He's calling from a borrowed phone, as usual. He lives in Kentucky and has spent the better part of his life walking the same Twelve Steps and the better part of the last decade living in halfway houses and under the occasional bridge. To hear my father speak playfully of a sturdy cardboard shanty he had built under an overpass in Louisville one night is a special kind of screwed up. But don't be fooled here. He is also a master manipulator who knows how to use language and intonation to elicit sympathy, and money, from others. It's been four months since we last spoke.

"What have you been up to, son? You still writing songs? Don't forget you get that from me," he says, blithely, in his thick southern drawl.

"Not much. Still driving, just workin' and helpin' Ma out. Josh is in jail again."

"Well, yeah. Okay, well I'll drop you a line again sometime soon. I love you!" "Yup." Click.

I haven't seen my father since I was 16, when I dropped out of high school and was sent to live with him and my grandfather in Kentucky because my mother no longer knew what to do with me. I landed a job bagging groceries and pushing carts at a supermarket alongside an old country woman named Frankie who would occasionally give me a joint or some speed during breaks. I was homesick, but my mother said I couldn't come home until I straightened up. I figured that if I got my GED, my mother would let me return home, so I began saving for the test. It didn't cost much, but I was only making $5.15 an hour—Kentucky's minimum wage at the time—and after having to buy my own groceries every week, pay for laundry and bus fare, and put money on my phone card to call home, I wasn't left with much to save. After a few months, though, I managed to save about $300—enough for the test and a bus ticket back to Massachusetts. I came home from work one night to discover it and my father missing. My father had found my hiding spot and had stolen all I'd saved. The apartment smelled like crack, plastic and noxious. He'd left his crack pipe on the bathroom sink. There was still a small white rock left in it, enough for another high, which meant he had gone to find more and he wanted to make sure that if he couldn't, he had at least one more high waiting for him at home. An incomplete combustion.

Or maybe I'm a black ox awakened to all things—awakened to how a gull feather folds over to white on a foamy shore as a hermeneutic fish chokes while no one is watching.

To prepare a body for cremation, a crematorium technician must first remove from the body any jewelry, silicone, mechanical prosthetics, or battery-operated medical devices. Failure to do so could result in an unwanted reaction, or an explosion.

A new company called Uber has made its way into town and has stolen the majority of our business, decimating the local taxi industry. My buddy offers me a job as a sternman on his lobster boat, HOUND DOG, which has been in his family for generations. "Day trips, so no being gone for weeks or months at a time, and depending on the haul, the pay is good. Lobsters are selling for $4 a pound right now and if we catch at least 2000 pounds, you could earn a grand a week."

"As the new guy, you'll be measuring and banding. You will put a metal gauge into the back of the lobster's eye socket and measure the distance to the end of its body. If the body is too small, you throw it back. If the body is too big, you throw it back. Inspect under its body. If you see eggs, cut a v-notch into its tail then throw it back. If you do not see eggs but see that there is a v-notch in the tail from a previous catch, this means that it is a known breeder and must be thrown back to ensure the survival of the population. Pick it up from behind, where it can't see you. If it manages to clamp onto one of your fingers, it will hurt but don't panic, just drop your hand to your side and it will slowly slide off. They don't like gravity. They're not used to it."

The cremated remains of an adult weigh 4-8 pounds. Metal urns and urns made from cultured materials are suitable for burial. Cultured materials include granite, marble, onyx, or custom blends of resin and filler that have the strength to withstand the underground forces which can cause physical stress to the urn over time.

I remove my hoodie, sneakers, and jeans and put on my brand new Grundens and white rubber waders. It's my first day on the boat. It's 4 AM and we reach the first trawl. I dunk a burlap sack into the ocean, wring it out, place it on the bottom of an empty cooler, then cover it with ice. The other sternmen are pulling up the trawl, a long string of knots and traps. There are twenty pots on this trawl, each overflowing with lobster. I can tell from the look on my buddy's face that this catch means that it has already been a good day. As the new guy tasked with measuring and banding, I take my station, position the cooler, and begin placing hundreds of rubber bands on hundreds of claws. After less than an hour, I fill the first large cooler. Packed tight with no wiggle room, each lobster lies flat with its tail tucked under its legs. I feel bad for them and think: "You will have a hard life. If this is where you are right now, you're going to have a hard rest of your life." I close the lid, wet another burlap sack, and rinse and prep the next cooler.

Or maybe I'm a stitcher of olive branches—a magician with a nightingale on a string of knots & a lover's perfumed linen note tucked square in a red handsewn pocket who ponders why, as we age, we rinse our straw clean.

I arrive home and get in the shower. What they don't tell you about working on a boat is that after you're done for the day, for a couple of hours at least, your body will still feel like it's listing back and forth. I place my hand on the wall as I shower, close my eyes, and try my best not to fall over. I'm burnt out, but I earned good money today.

If you're still unsure about whether cremation is the right choice, we've put together an article that compares the features of cremations and burials. You'll be able to compare the costs, procedures, and various benefits of each type of service below.

It's 6 PM and I should get to sleep. I'm going out again tomorrow and if I'm not at the dock at 3 AM sharp, they'll leave without me. I sit down on my bed, sharpen a pencil, and finish the poem. A complete combustion:

String of Knots

In burnt-ivory morning air, an ensouled plume
inks the sky from the chimney of a stone crematory
on a hill in the woods. Once a fragile container
of memories to come, now an obsidian crest
to the knowable world—a lumpy, decanted
moment—how time appears as change
appears. In my mind tucked safe, I think—
Maybe I will be this image to a future
poet. No—I'll be a sapphire vessel
transcending the sense-world that only exists
because it once was versed, once was imaged
like a tortoise shell full of proverbs or foxglove
in orange-vanilla nightfall. Or maybe I'm a black ox
awakened to all things—awakened
to how a gull feather folds over to white on a foamy
shore as a hermeneutic fish chokes while no one
is watching. Or maybe I'm a stitcher of olive branches—
a magician with a nightingale on a string of knots
& a lover's perfumed linen note
tucked square in a red handsewn pocket who ponders
why, as we age, we rinse our straw clean.
I imagine this smoke—once a man, or woman,
or child even, with dimples—& watch as he,
she, or the little one touches the dawn high

as snowflakes poke through the sooty vestige
of what it means to be human & I wonder if I,
or anyone I know, should be so lucky
& I light a new fire at the end of myself.

Even After I Die,
I Will Hear Your Words and Remain

As a poet writing from within peculiar spaces these days—from within *lost*, perhaps, as lost is a place, not always negative—I find myself ruminating on poets writing to one another, speaking to and answering one another, through space and time. Susan Briante's *Defacing the Monument* reminds me—in a metaphysical way vis-à-vis deepening a conversation—of Rossetti's claim that "a sonnet is a moment's monument." Like sonnets, many documents are framed by a recognizable form, structure, or authoritarianism by their very definitions alone. What happens to the direction of a written conversation or the document thereof if the conversation is removed from its preinstalled form, structure, or authoritarianism? It not only extends itself but speaks itself backward.

"What ruins are you writing through, or writing with?"— Briante

In thinking of the spatial and temporal dimensions of dead poets speaking to future dead poets who've yet to be born, I must speak to an ongoing conversation I'm currently having with dear friend and long-dead poet, Rubén Darío.

"Who walks that field with me ... To whom does it belong ...
How can I continue on my path without harming any potential
you?" — Briante

If Time is a monument that our species has built from within itself, then language is how we alter the appearance of the door to this monument, to step outside Time's form, structure, and authoritarianism. When we step outside of our monument, outside Time, we enter the field, we enter the field with others—*others* being those who've already died and transcended Time—and together we forge a path of carefully chosen conversations, conversations that, for the most part, are formed from sentences that will not to cause harm to the potentialities of our experience; i.e., words that we find on the path that fit in our pockets, words that have been charged with new meaning and therefore able to enter or reenter the monument of Time with new purpose. Rubén Darío's pockets are filled with these words. He writes to me, during a moment of readerly revelation:

Even after I die, I will hear your words and remain.
If you do well, I'll applaud. If you don't, you'll be disgraced.
I'll be a harp to sing you, the alb's cord around your waist.
Think of me as your navel or living inside your brain.
—from "To a Poet"

Darío spent his life utterly terrified of death, and due to this, he found immortality in words.

He spent his life defacing the meaning of mortality. I do not write this lightly. When he, and other poets like him, call on posterity, it is posterity's duty to step outside the monument of Time and extend the conversation. We are called to reply. I reply:

for Rubén Darío

I've seen the divine cantharus
adrift white in the tide's navel
buoyant and brazenly moved
by its own movement—

Even after you died, you heard its words
and remained

a true rhapsodomancy in the shape
of a heart.

Your melancholy was cut from Argo's white sail
first pierced by the dart of a nocturne still sung
by your celestial bull.

The azure cord around the alb's waist remains
tied to the star that blessed my brain's reveries.

Time is a ruin we write through; its poems are the ruins we write with.

A Cup Full of Tongues Crossing Their Legs

I've spent the past few months dealing with dental issues, getting fillings and crowns. I've always felt uncomfortable by the amount of artificial substances that are permanently in my mouth, from the unnatural feel of cheap fillings against my tongue to the substance used in filling an old root canal. After having read *Lightning Flowers* by Katherine E. Standefer, I was inspired to research the materials in my teeth. Most of us know about the dangers in metal fillings, but I was most surprised by the substance used for root canals. It turns out that root canals rely on a substance called *gutta-percha*, a "tough thermoplastic substance which is the coagulated latex of certain Malaysian trees." I have learned that *gutta-percha* was once used by Malaysian natives to make knife handles and walking sticks. In the Western world, it has been used to make furniture, golf balls, rifle shoulder pads, and canes, and it has also been used as insulating material for undersea telegraph cables. I have never been to Malaysia, but I have carried the chemically modified sap from its trees in my mouth for over a decade. *Lightning Flowers* begs me to consider deeply how the violence of a substance upon its retrieval remains in the substance. My dental issues are of course trivial compared to what Katherine Standefer carries inside her. I could live without teeth, if I had to.

In this response, I must also consider poetry, as the act of writing poetry is the act of following an object to its source. Poetry is a substance—albeit intangible—that forms within the poet's senses, and don't poets write poetry to get a bit closer to its origin, learning along the way that it is a substance that is ever-originating from within? Standefer writes: "That to make basically anything require[s] earth." As a human, I am part of the earth, my body could not live without Earth, thus what I make requires me. I am reminded here that my poetry requires me.

In 2013, I was just beginning to study poetry full time. I was new to poetry (still am, always will be) and was attempting, after much work in repetition and mimesis, to unearth my own voice. Children learn through repetition, but I hit a plateau, so I asked for my own voice. One night, in a hypnagogic state, a line appeared in my mind, clairvoyantly: *A cup full of tongues crossing their legs.* This line, the experience of receiving it, gave me my voice, or at least, the door to what would later become my first poetic vocabulary. At the time, I had no idea what the line could mean, but a professor with whom I shared it told me that it sounded "surreal" and that I should study Surrealism. I was to begin at its source: André Breton's *Surrealist Manifesto* (1929). I experienced a profound synchronicity in learning that the surrealist movement originated from a line of poetry that Breton had received while in a hypnagogic state, clairvoyantly. Breton's line: *There is a man cut in two by the window.* The appearance of this line in Breton's mind drove him into a beautiful madness, one which birthed Surrealism. Surrealism, as we've known it for nearly a century, would not exist if it were not for Breton's obsessive curiosity, and I am forever grateful that he recorded his experience. I like to believe that, somewhere in the æther, a man cut in two by the window is holding a cup full of tongues crossing their legs.

Rodent in the Machine

This week, after a year-and-a-half sans vehicle post-COVID, I purchased a car. All was well with the car until yesterday, when the check engine light came on. This surprised me, as it had just passed inspection and was running flawlessly. I know cars, and knew that the error code pointed to a lean fuel/air mixture, meaning that one should first check the air filter and surrounding vacuum hoses. I removed the air filter from the engine compartment and discovered a handful of oak leaves stuffed alongside a small brown field mouse. I stood in shock, not because I could not believe that a mouse had made its way in there—this is known to happen—but because the big-eared mouse looked like it was happily sleeping, curled in a fetal position next to its nest of leaves. I had not owned this machine for more than a week and it had already killed something.

My heart immediately sank into the sight of this creature, but my mind was immediately relieved, considering that I had discovered the car's problem and would not have to spend any money to fix it, money I didn't have, since the check engine light disappeared once the mouse-clog was removed. In this moment, as I was simultaneously torn between emotion and logic, I felt choked by the divisiveness of life. This dead mouse, this *rodent* to most others, had in an instant become a symbol for what it meant to dwell in the space between nature and machine, proclaiming with its big dead ears that *machine* often wins. I own this machine. I own the need for it. We all do. I promptly buried the mouse under some small gray stones nearby and thanked it for what it had taught me.

I recall here the poem "These Hands, If Not Gods" by Natalie Diaz. Upon first read, I mistakenly experienced the word "Gods" as the possessive "God's." It was not until after I'd buried the mouse and returned to the poem that I realized the word was "Gods" and that my hands—in those moments of driving, unknowingly killing, then burying—were unseen Gods to that mouse, but not God's. The opening line of the seventh stanza stays with me: "Aren't they, too, the dark carpenters/ of your small church?"

Humankind lives in the space between nature and machine, between the language of nature and the machine through which we share our language with others, through the machine on which these words are being written. And as a poet, I dwell in the kitchen of language-making, breaking bread with poetry and poets future past, but now I can hear the mice in the kitchen, skittering through crumbs on the floor, en route to a seemingly safe nest tucked deep in the unforgiving engine of things.

Scholarly Critiques

The Hidden Numerology of T.S. Eliot's "The Waste Land"

In section one, "The Burial of the Dead," one finds the element *earth* in "the dead land"; "roots"; "Earth"; "mountains"; "branches"; "tree"; "cricket"; "stone"; "rock"; "garden"; "city"; "feet"; "corpse"; and in the actions of "sprout" and "bloom." Numerologically, one finds 3 in "three staves"; 1 in "one-eyed merchant"; and 9 in "the final stroke of nine." In numerology, these numbers together become the number 4. The mystic relationship between 4 and *earth* is evidenced in nature's four elements, four directions, and four seasons. In Tarot, the number 4 symbolizes stability and security, or having one's "feet on the ground." Biblically, the creation of the material universe was completed on the fourth day, when God created the sun, moon, and stars. For the reader, the 4-*earth* of this section resides in both the literal and psychic space between the "shadow behind" and the "shadow rising."

In section two, "A Game of Chess," one finds the element *air* in "strange synthetic perfumes ... the sense in odours; stirred by the air"; "smoke"; the "inviolable voice" and "Jug Jug" of the nightingale; in the repetition of "wind" within the context of a dialogue suspended and spaced airy-like on the page; in the "O O O O" of the Shakespearean Rag song; and finally, in the notion of someone returning (Albert). Numerologically, one finds the number 14 in "Doubled the flames of sevenbranched candelabra"; 10 in "the hot water at ten"; 4 in "a closed car at four"; 4 again in "four years"; 31 in Lil's age; and 5 in "She's had five already." In numerology, these numbers together become the number 5. In numerology, the mystic relationship between the number 5 and *air* is evidenced in spiritual circles as symbolizing desire for freedom, movement and motion, independence, and change. In Tarot, the number 5 symbolizes the human being in both its human and spiritual forms and this means, succinctly, acceptance of imperfection. Biblically, 5 symbolizes a human being's five fingers, five toes, and aptly, the five great mysteries: Father, Son, Spirit, Creation, and Redemption. For the reader, the 5-*air* of this section can be experienced in the refrain "HURRY UP PLEASE ITS TIME." One should note, too, how the "ITS" here is not the apostrophied conjunction of *it is* as one would expect, so the "ITS" here may allude to something that possesses the time.

An aside: I was at first tempted to equate section two to the *spirit/ aether* element, as the etymology of the word *chess*, in Persian, comes from "SHAH," meaning "King," with the original version of the word SHAH being "ASHA," meaning The Cosmic Order (*spirit/aether*). "Chess" also of course as an allusion to the game of life, Fate vs Free Will, etc., but this would have removed the element from the natural (or supranatural) order of its being—the elements in this order would not flow in their correct spiritual or natural order if structured as *earth, spirit/aether, fire, water, air*, thus further proving Eliot's intentions of sectioning "The Waste Land" under the natural law of cosmic order.

In section three, "The Fire Sermon," one of course finds the element *fire* not only in the title, but also in the extinguishing of things: in the nymphs in their departure; in the "ended" song; in the "cigarette ends"; and the "no addresses"—these things have all run their course, much as fire eventually does. One proceeds to find *fire*, quite cleverly, in the "slimy belly on the bank." Though the "slimy belly" here is in reference to a rat, one cannot help but think of the "slimy belly" of the fire-resistant alchemical salamander, as the salamander is a prominent symbol of fire and of the *Prima Materia*—the formless base of all matter (quintessence or aether), which wonderfully marries the essence of section two to the opening of section three here, a transmutation if you will (also evidenced in "The wind crosses the brown land, unheard.). One would surely equate a "slimy belly" to a salamander before they would a rat, further proving the hidden symbolism within the line. One could, however, also equate the rat with *fire* if one recalls the rat's role in The Black Plague, as the rat-disease "consumed" over 100 million lives. One continues to find *fire* in the "motor" and "engine;" in "moon shone bright"; in the lighting of a stove; the "sun's last rays"; "Ionian white and gold"; "red and gold"; and climatically in the "Burning burning burning burning/ ... pluckest me out/ ... Thou pluckest/ burning" of the closing lines.

Numerologically, one finds 2 in "two lives"; 1 in "one bold stare"; 1 in "one final patronising kiss"; and 1 again in "one half-formed thought." In numerology, these numbers together become the number 5. This further proves the marrying of the elements section by section, as the reappearance or continuance of 5 here mirrors the movement of *fire* from *air*. Symbolically, *fire* shares with *air* the same attributes of 5 as a symbol of freedom, movement and motion, independence, change, the five great mysteries, etc. (and the ability to cause destruction). This elemental marriage is complete in the closing "Burning burning burning burning/ ... pluckest me out/ ... Thou pluckest/ burning," as both fire and air are the two elements of this destruction—a fire cannot exist without air, thus the mystic joining of both elements is essenced in the 5-5 of *fire* and *air*, sections two and sections three. As one would expect, this fiery marriage is destroyed only by *water*.

In section four, "Death by Water," one finds the element *water* in all the right places: in the title of course, followed by the "deep sea swell"; "the current under sea"; the "whirlpool"; and in the general flow of the section, in the "rose and fell" (as with the previous sections, the flow of this section could be thought to mirror its element.). The structure of the section's indentations reflects the ebb and flow, a brief wave on which the eye of the reader can surf. There are no numbers in this section (the 14 of "fortnight" does not count, as it is a length of time and not a specified number here); however, if one looks at the section number, number 4, we are taken back to the 4-*earth* of section one as well as to the 5-*air* of section two, which Eliot suggests the reader does: "O you who turn the wheel and look to windward." Eliot is telling the reader here to face the wind, to face *air* and the number 5, which possibly leads one to feel as if they are walking backward toward the next section, section five.

In the fifth and final section of the poem, "What the Thunder Said," one finds *spirit/aether* in the ineffable images and effects of "torchlight red on sweaty faces"; "frosty silence in the garden"; "agony of stone places"; "reverberation"; "thunder"; and in the long list of things which *are but are not* in the second and third stanzas. One continues to find *spirit/aether* in the ghostly "third who walks always beside you" up ahead on the "white road"; in that which is neither "a man or a woman"; in the "sound high in the air"; the "city over the mountains;" the "violet" air and light (longing/grief); the "unreal" and "upside down,"; in the ghostly "voices singing out of empty cisterns and exhausted wells"; in "a flash of lightning"; "empty rooms"; "aethereal rumours"; and finally, in the "sea" of a "heart" "beating obedient" its "fragments" of prayer onto the sacred floor of the poem, an ending which offers not a transcendence, rather a turning back to section one's *earth*, a cycle of the elements which could seem complete on paper, but are not.

Numerologically, one finds 3 in "the third who walks always beside you" and 1 in "turn once only." (One must omit the other "one"s and "once"s in this section, as these reference a person and a past period of time, not the number 1 in its numerical form, as in "one time" or "one person.") In numerology, these numbers together become the number 4. This mirrors section four's 4-*water* mirroring section one's 4-*earth*, and one is reminded here of the mystic relationship of *spirit/aether* to the watery movement or fluidity of ghosts and Spirit in connection to the earthly realm—humankind's ability to be born (earth), to flourish (air), to destruct (fire), to die and return to the abyss (water), to haunt or transcend (spirit/aether).

To summarize "The Waste Land" numerologically: it holds a spiritual rhythm of 4-5-5-4-4, and when broken down to its purest numerological form, "The Waste Land" is the number 4—a psychic environment of the four base elements of materiality not yet imbued with divine *spirit/aether*, its four directions ever-attempting to point back to the beginning and end of their purgatory, suspended in the limbo of number 4, stuck on the fourth day of creation, when the material universe is completed but still bereft of God's image, fertility, and rejuvenation. It is important to note, too, that the standalone question of "Who is the third who always walks beside you?" is the poem itself recognizing its imminent, abrupt end. Further, "Who is the third who always walks beside you?" is line number 360. In numerology, this line becomes the number 9, which can be thought to have been prophesied in "on the final stroke of nine" in the *fourth* stanza of the poem.

On Emily Dickinson's
"The Poets light but Lamps —"

As a poet, I'm at home in Dickinson's poem, "The Poets light but Lamps —." The poem prompts a consideration of divine mystery, of what it means to explore one's life and lineage through metaphor. The poem asks me to explore and honor my own relationship to poetry and its lineage, as it conjures the deeply satisfying image of one writing a poem at 3 AM by candlelight, of one attempting to make sense of the chaos of the world, as it sleeps, through language.

The poem begs to interrogate what it means to be a poet who has never married or had children (poems are the childless poet's children, after all). As a poet who has also never married or had children, I see Dickinson's "lamps" as a metaphor for the poems I will leave for posterity. I think of my body eventually dying as a "go[ing] out." I know the divine essences behind a true poem as the "wicks" I stimulate (with the help of the muses, of course). "If vital light" asks me if writing poetry is as necessary to my life as its "suns" are to my days (it is). I see "Each Age a Lens/ Disseminating their/ Circumference —" as the poets of the past, and as myself looking at my own place on poetry's thread.

"The Poets light but Lamps —" is an action of mirrors, as Dickinson uses symbol and intellect to explore the beauty and melancholy of what it means to be a poet who will leave only poems to the world. The poem evokes in me a truth of how a poet's life is both enough and never enough.

The Distance of Grief Becomes Purple

I have been ruminating over Paul Celan's "Psalm" for the last couple of weeks. As a poet interested in Hermeticism in twentieth-century poetry, Celan's name appears quite often in my notes, and although I have yet to thoroughly meditate in the lush garden of his work, I intuit that "Psalm" is a good place to start.

The title "Psalm" creates a polarizing effect on the spiritual senses, as the poem reads as both a Psalm and anti-Psalm in its essence, particularly when one considers Psalm 34 ("Let us exalt his name together ... The righteous cry out, and the Lord hears them") and Psalm 37 (My servants the righteous, shall inherit the earth"). Since the word *psalm* itself does not appear within the body of the poem, it is difficult to know whether Celan offers the poem as a *Psalm*—the capitalized biblical or spiritual version of the word—or as a *psalm*, the indiscriminate lowercase version. Since Celan was known for criticizing religious structures, and since he had a history of navigating tensions within his Jewish roots, one could presuppose that Celan wrote "Psalm" as an anti-Psalm.

Upon first read, one can see that "flower," "flowering," and "no one's rose" are coupled with the heliotropic action of "we shall flower/ Towards/ you," which could establish an image of sunflowers as "no one's rose," since sunflowers are heliotropic and grow toward the sun, but when one arrives at the closing stanza, the anthropomorphized flowers are revealed to not be sunflowers, rather actual roses—Celan's "no one's rose"—with their "corolla red," "crimson word," and "thorn." On first reading Michael Hamburger's translation, I was a bit addled by the line "our corolla red/ with the crimson word which we sang." Something about "corolla red" being two syllables away from "crimson" baffled me. With the chance to elaborate upon the imagery of the flowers and their actions in the closing stanza, why choose two shades of the same color? I intuited that this was not Celan's intention but rather a byproduct of what can often get lost in translation. Compelled to seek other translations, I discovered that I was correct in my intuition. In the original poem, written in German, Celan uses the word, "Purpurwort," a word that Hamburger translates to "crimson word." In German, *Purpurwort* means "purple word." Other English translations of Celan's "Purpurwort" appear true to form as purpleword, Violet-Word, etc. How does the essence or poetic power of "Psalm" change when the metaphor of the flower sings purple rather than crimson words over its thorns?

While the color purple often conjures images of royalty and abundance (Ovid's "no cover dyed with the juice of purple berries"), it may also conjure images of exile and displacement. Two examples come to mind from our readings thus far: purple appears in Wallace Stevens' "Tea at the Palaz of Hoon," in the opening line "Not less because in purple I descended"; as well as in Anthony Hecht's "Exile," in the image of "The purplish clinkers near the cinder blocks/ that support the steps of an abandoned church/ still moored to a telephone pole."

Emily Dickinson, as we know, was spiritually displaced, and she incorporated "purple" into more than fifty of her poems. The color purple, to Dickinson, often represented (or seemed to represent) feelings of grief and expansion. To Dickinson, the distance of grief becomes purple, a color that would reflect back to her both that which she could not spiritually escape nor die into. It seems that Celan, Stevens, and Hecht possibly utilize the color purple in much the same way as Dickinson, at least in the aforementioned lines. Of course, I am making a generalization gleaned from only a handful of lines, but one cannot help but wonder what drove these poets, in their moments of poetic revelation, to envision the color purple within the context of their grief.

One could consider poetry a closer reality, while one could also consider poetry a displacement from reality, or at times, its ghostprint. Poets share these close realities with readers, but in thinking of how poems have the power to speak to one another, could it be rational to consider that poets share amongst themselves a collective consciousness of displacement? If so, one could easily envision a purpling horizon from a psychic landscape on which an exiled poetics has long taken root.

On Elizabeth Bishop's "The Moose"

Elizabeth Bishop's poem "The Moose" begs me to once again think of color in poetry (or perhaps a psychological or phenomenological *poetics of color*). In "The Moose," color is utilized twelve times: brown, red, red, red, pink, pink, blue, white, gray, white, whitewashed, and red, respectively. One could often assume with poetry that color is simply a color, a necessary adjective that better details an image to the reader, but other times, color in a poem becomes more than an adjective, it becomes a curious palette weaved (thinking of the etymology of the word *text* here)—consciously or unconsciously—into the poem as a means of alchemizing the images in ways that keep the poem moving, or transmuting. I am thinking of an analogy of a clock here: If the poem (text) is the face of a clock, then the rhythm of the poem is the clock's hands, while the adjectives (color, here) are some of the gears which keep the hands, or poem, in motion. It is easy for one to pull meaning from thin air when it comes to interpreting color in poetry, but there are connections between color, emotion, and the senses in "The Moose" that are worth exploring.

One begins to experience the color of the poem in "brown foam," then journeys through the images of a red bay, a red sea, red gravelly roads, a "windshield flashing pink," "pink glancing off of metal," "blue, beat-up enamel," white feathers, "gray glazed cabbages," "wet white string," "whitewashed fences," finally settling into the glow of "a red light [that] swims through the dark." The reader's psyche is left with the residual color of the red light as they proceed through the next sixteen stanzas sans color (imagining for themselves the color of the schooner, the dog, and the shawl). The thread of color here, the poem's *palette*, seems to anchor itself to the surprised, perplexed question of "Why, why do we feel/ (we all feel) this sweet/ sensation of joy?" The speaker's unexpected "sweet sensation of joy"—while the tone simultaneously mirrors a loss of joy ("Goodbye to the elms ... ")—can be seen and felt as an arch of color, which begins to trail off in the fumes of the moment's end at the closing line, in the "acrid/ smell of gasoline." Thus, there is a base, earth (or brown) in "of fish and bread and tea," and, as the poem rises to its meaning, it descends to a close in the form of ascension.

Could this palette represent the motion of the sensation of displacement (an interior safety startled by a juxtaposition of the exterior) as anchored to the surprising experience of joy? Could one see the speaker's emotional journey here as a cyclical return to a base emotion, in general and perhaps, in a way, synesthetically? It could. It could not. Regardless, it is an interesting glimpse into the inner workings of the essence of the poem.

In thinking of a more concrete symbol of exile in Bishop's work, one could explore the symbol of the turtle in "Crusoe in England." "Turtle" appears four times throughout the poem, conjuring the image of Crusoe's turtles. As we know, Crusoe "found a large turtle or tortoise," and upon preparing to cook it the next day, found inside the female turtle "three-score eggs," or sixty eggs. Crusoe ate the eggs over time, and eventually found "innumerable turtles" on the island, which Bishop mirrors throughout her metaphors. The turtle itself is a symbol of exile. It is a solitary creature that is only found in groups if the environment of the place permits, and even then, they are unsocial. For this reason, the turtle can be thought of as the animal-symbol of the hermit or hermetess, and it is sometimes placed in the environment of the hermit or hermetess in poetry and literature (more on this in a later paper). One recalls lines from Mary Robinson's poem, "Anselmo, The Hermit of the Alps," where Robinson writes: "The lonely turtle's plaintive moan/ Recall'd her song's celestial tone;/ And ev'ry dew-drop, trembling near,/ Gave to his soul -- her parting tear!" (On a personal note, this reflection reminds me of when I have used these symbols together in one of my older poems: "a hermit dismantles saturnian charms/ by an empty river/ breaks bread with a lemon-colored turtle/ belly-up.")

In "Crusoe in England," the turtles "lumber by," and then there are "more turtles," there are "hissing, ambulating turtles" which "got on my nerves." I now turn to J. E. Cirlot's *A Dictionary of Symbols*, where Cirlot writes:

> In every case, the turtle is a symbol of material existence and not of any aspect of transcendence, for even where it is a combination of square and circle it alludes to the forms of the manifest world and not to the creative forces, nor to the Origin, still less to the irradiating Centre. In view of its slowness, it might be said to symbolize natural evolution ... it is an emblem of longevity ... the turtle is the inversion of wings ... since the wings signify elevation of the spirit, the turtle would denote the fixed element of alchemy [*massa confusa*] although only in its negative aspect. In short, then, it would stand for turgidity, involution, obscurity, slowness, stagnation and highly concentrated materialism, etc.

Cirlot's assertions here seem to ring true to Bishop's use of (or borrowing of) the symbol. Bishop writes "I couldn't bear to think what size/ the goats and turtles were," suggesting a spiritual or emotional heaviness or stagnation when thinking of the turtle. She continues, "The turtles lumbered by, high-domed ... I'd turn. And they'd prove/ to be more turtles," further implying the symbol as a fixed element of the journey, a "concentrated materialism" of the turgid inner and outer realms. One then reaches the climax of the symbol in "hissing, ambulating turtles" that "got on my nerves," suggesting that the speaker could take no more, further evidenced by the proceeding "I'd shut my eyes and think about a tree,/ an oak, say, with real shade, somewhere." The desire for "real shade" is a longing for transcendence, a longing to take flight, but since the turtle is the inversion of wings, the longing, and exhaustion, are not remedied. The poem further proves its materiality in the closing stanzas, where the reader is left with weighty, somber images of a knife, a museum, death, disease, and a chunk of time.

Deep on the Bone of Experience

In surveying my inclination to collect symbols and images of exile and displacement from recent readings, I have come to realize that I have been searching for Moore's "real toads in imaginary gardens." While I intend to add more toads to my bucket over the coming years, the origin of Cædmon's Hymn urges me to pause for a moment to consider the gardens from which some of the most curious toads have appeared. An aside: It is fascinating how Moore—or who she quotes in her poem—chooses toad over frog in her metaphor, since toads can survive on dry land and frogs cannot, which begs one to consider the page as a dry environment for poetry, as opposed to the wet or "fluid" environment of oracular poetry when recited from the mouth.

Cædmon's Hymn, unlike most poems, is not an imaginary garden with real toads in it; Cædmon's Hymn, in its entirety, *is* the toad, and the garden is the dream from whence it hopped. We know that many poems throughout history have come to us as byproducts of divine dream experience, and with this in mind, I have been thinking about Cædmon's Hymn in relation to André Breton. I have also been thinking about the famed line from "Amazing Grace," "I once was lost, but now am found," in relation to how a poem itself can be the primary object of displacement for the poet, and of how the experience of having one's poem translated further displaces the poem from the poet.

Some write that Cædmon was visited by a woman in his dream, while others write that he was visited by a man. Gender and socio-historical contexts aside, Bede wrote that Cædmon was visited by "someone" (*quidam*), so one must approach Cædmon's Hymn with this in mind, knowing that all we know from the first translation is that Cædmon supposedly had an experience of being visited in a dream by an ambiguous divine presence who asked him to sing. Regardless, due to Cædmon's dream experience, words spilled onto the living world, words that forever positioned Cædmon to become the first known English poet of the first known English poem.

In his *Manifeste du Surréalisme*, André Breton writes that the idea of Surrealism came to him one night while in a hypnagogic dreamstate, when "There is a man cut in two by the window" appeared suddenly in his mind as a visual phrase. Breton took "There is a man cut in two by the window" to mean that the conscious and subconscious realms of human experience could coexist as a *surreality*. This dream experience became the catalyst for Breton to establish one of the most famous artistic and literary movements of the modern world. Surrealism, though it had followed Dadaism, would likely not exist as we have known it if Breton did not have this dream, just as Cædmon's Hymn would not exist if Cædmon did not have his dream. We know that there are a number of examples of this, especially in the ancient world, but one cannot help but ask: In these fantastic instances, do these movements or poems thereof create *themselves* through a divine need to be born into our world at a certain time by seeking those who happen to be attuned to their metaphysical frequency? If so, could one posit that Cædmon's Hymn displaced *itself* from its cosmic origin by giving itself to Cædmon, and ultimately humankind, in a dream? Could Surrealism's overflowing bucket of "toads" have been exiled from creation's cosmic energy to the psychic automatism of Surrealist poetry and art? Of course, I am bypassing "muse" here, along with the human act of putting the thing out into the world, but I cannot help but think at this moment that a poem is not just an act of human expression, but also a fundamental act of creation that refigures itself through the poet for the sake of a cyclical cosmic self-remembrance ("In the beginning was the Word"). This would help to explain why poetry continues to thrive in a world that no longer rewards poetry monetarily. And perhaps this is what Moore means when she writes that there is "a perfect contempt for it," when one feels more a slave to poetry than its master.

Although this reflection asks a number of ontological questions best suited for phenomenological criticism rather than literary criticism, and while I have yet to study Blake's spiritual visions in relation, I intuit that Wordsworth's "Expostulation and Reply," upon a few more close reads, may very well answer some of my questions, particularly in stanza six, where he writes, "'Nor less I deem that there are Powers/ Which of themselves our minds impress;/ That we can feed this mind of ours/ In a wise passiveness."

I chose to bring Breton in relation to Cædmon here because the theme of a poet being born from a divine dream resonates deeply and profoundly with me. With respect to the process, and at the dutiful risk of coming across as objectively unhinged: I experienced a dream one night, in 2014, where a black and white photo of a man's face flashed in my mind "out of nowhere," along with a name I psychically "knew" to be "Ruben." This felt important enough in my dreamstate to jar me awake. I quickly turned to Google Images and began searching for the photo I had seen in my dream, typing "Ruben" into the search engine. (In my deep dreamstate, I remember holding onto the thought of "Ruben name not the sandwich," as I felt that I was being guided to search for this online, and that I would have to input the term "-sandwich" into the search engine to better pinpoint the results). After a few moments of scrolling down the webpage through a sea of unknown faces, I saw the exact photo that appeared to me in my dream. The photo was of a poet named Rubén Darío. In a state of spiritual shock, I went to the page linked to the photo and was taken to a poem written in Spanish, where the only word I could understand in the poem was "Jason," my first name (Argonauts, in the context of the poem). Within the span of only a few minutes, I experienced a flash of a man's photo in my dream, somehow knew his first name, awoke, then found my first name staring back at me from a poem he had written over one hundred years earlier. With absolute certainty, I had never seen this photo nor heard of this man beforehand; this was not cryptomnesia. This dream experience, I can now solemnly declare, is what indelibly altered the course of my life and led me to where I am today—it was Poetry inviting me into its lineage.

To recall the theme of exile and displacement in poetry, it is important to note that Darío was displaced numerous times in numerous ways throughout his life—spiritually, poetically, politically, and even geographically, from his family and his homeland.

On the next page, the photo of Darío I had first seen in that dream, alongside one of the first translated poems of his I had read shortly thereafter, now forever etched in *azur* ink deep on the bone of experience which, for lack of a more fitting phrase, beautifully haunts the living hell out of me:

To a Poet
(Fragment)

Even after I die, I will hear your words and remain.
If you do well, I'll applaud. If you don't, you'll be disgraced.
I'll be a harp to sing you, the alb's cord around your waist.
Think of me as your navel or living inside your brain

Alchemy and Hermeticism in 'Aṭṭār's *Book of God*: Discourse I and Discourse XIX

This essay seeks to deduce that Farīd al-Dīn 'Aṭṭār, the famed 12th-century Iranian mystic poet, incorporated metaphors of the seven alchemical stages of transformation and the seven Hermetic principles into his poetic discourses, metaphors which on the surface may seem to only allude to the seven veils or seven levels of being in Sufi philosophy. I will seek to expound that even though certain metaphors are centered on the seven veils or seven levels of being in Sufi philosophy, they are also centered on, or synergistically encoded with, the principles and stages of Hermetic-alchemical philosophy, which in themselves serve to shift the reader's consciousness toward a space of spiritual or mystical experience. For this study, I refer to *The Ilahi-nama, or, Book of God of Farīd al-Dīn 'Aṭṭār*, as translated by John Andrew Boyle. I will explore Discourse I in relation to the seven Hermetic principles, followed by Discourse XIX in relation to the seven stages of alchemical transformation.

'Aṭṭār was a master mystic poet as well as the son of a chemist, and it is said that he worked as pharmacist before allegedly abandoning the career to travel extensively and commit his life to the Sufi path. 'Aṭṭār lived and traveled in the 12th and 13th centuries (CE 1145 – 1221), during the peak of alchemical practice in India and the Islamic world, just before alchemy reached its height in Europe in the Middle Ages around CE 1300. Given 'Aṭṭār's background in chemistry and pharmacology during a period when Hermeticism and alchemy were practiced far and wide—and given the fact that 'Aṭṭār directly mentions alchemy and the Philosopher's Stone quite often throughout his discourses—I assert that it was not only possible but probable that 'Aṭṭār consciously or subconsciously encoded these philosophies within Sufi philosophy in order to offer his readers a dynamic mosaic of Mystery, or secret teachings, which in and of themselves exist to reveal their encodement only to those who seek them or who are thought to be sought by them.

As Rafal Stepien writes:

> The understanding here is that "The primary intention of the poet in these poems is to express the various mystical stations, states and interactions" ... 'Aṭṭār was supposedly not at all interested in poetry as an art form, which was thus consigned to merely harbouring all the rhetorical flourishes characteristic of the verbose outpourings of his contemporaries. Rather, his sole purpose in turning to the composition of poetry was to expedite the pilgrimage of his fellow man towards his one true end.[1]

Stepien allows us to consider that if 'Aṭṭār's poetic motivation was in fact centered on expressing and exploring *various* mystical stations, states, and interactions, then one cannot prove that 'Aṭṭār did not encode the seven stages of alchemical transformation and the seven Hermetic principles within his discourses, particularly if 'Aṭṭār's intention was to use whichever dynamic theopoetic subjects were both necessary and available at the time to achieve his goal of enlightening his readership. I will now turn to the opening scene of Discourse I, offered below in its entirety, which I believe 'Aṭṭār encoded with the seven Hermetic principles. In this deconstruction, I aim to show how 'Aṭṭār reveals to the reader each one of the seven Hermetic principles in their respective order.

Discourse I

One who had traveled the world and lost his friends, a man bewildered of heart and disturbed of mind,
    Had the tale from a man who knew thereof that once a certain caliph had six sons.

---

1   See Stepien, Rafal. "A Study in Sufi Poetics: The Case of 'Aṭṭār Nayshābūrī." Oriens, vol. 41, no. 1/2, 2013, pp. 77–120. p. 84.

All were by nature of lofty ambition and had not dismissed feelings of pride from their minds.

Of all the sciences of their time they were each without peer in every one.

Since they were each of them masters of the arts of this world, since each of them was an Adam in both worlds,

Their father made them sit together one day. 'You are all', he said, 'conversant with the knowledge of the world.

You are a caliph's sons, you are kings—what does each of you ask of the world?

If you have a hundred wishes or if but one, tell me, each of you.

When I know how each of you thinks I will order the affairs of each in accordance with his desire.'

One of the princes was the first to reveal his secret. 'It is related', he said, 'by the great and eminent

That the king of the peris has a virgin daughter to whom the moon cannot be compared.

She is as beautiful as the mind and as delicate as the soul. She is the fairest in earth or heaven.

If I can entirely realize this wish, it is all I crave until Judgment Day.

Being with such a beauty how should anyone seek any perfection beyond this?

He that is near to the sun, how should he wish for a single beam?

Such is my desire, and if I have it not, nothing but madness shall be my faith.'

Father's reply

The father said: 'Beware of lust, for with lust thou art very drunk.

When a man's heart is imprisoned in venery, all the coin of his being will be spent.

But every woman who is manlike in her conduct is a complete stranger to such lust,

Just as that woman who was separated from her husband became the leader of men in the court of God.' [2]

The seven Hermetic principles, as originally appearing in *The Kybalion*[3], are Mentalism, Correspondence, Vibration, Polarity, Rhythm, Cause and Effect, and Gender, respectively, and are considered the great Universal Laws. In the opening lines of Discourse I, we read that there is "a man bewildered of heart and disturbed of mind ... All were by nature of lofty ambition," which alludes to the first Hermetic principle, The Principle of Mentalism. The Principle of Mentalism dictates that "All is mind" and teaches that everything in the material universe, everything in one's outward reality, is part of a universal living mind and that everything material, whether animate or inanimate, is produced by one's psychic energy through thought.[4] 'Aṭṭār is initiating the "bewildered" reader here and introducing them to their own mind, hence the repetition of the word "mind."

The next lines in Discourse I, "Of all the sciences of their time they were each without peer in every one. Since they were each of them masters of the arts of this world, since each of them was an Adam in both worlds," alludes to the second Hermetic principle, The Principle of Correspondence. The Principle of Correspondence introduces the now well-known phrase, "As above, so below; as below, so above,"[5] and teaches that one must intelligently move between the known and unknown and that every *thing* responds to every other *thing* simultaneously and under Universal Law. This principle also recalls the tearing-away of the veil of Isis in order to catch a glimpse of the goddess. 'Aṭṭār writes that each son

2   'Aṭṭār, Farīd al-Dīn, and John Andrew Boyle. *The Ilahi-Nama, or, Book of God of Farīd Al-Dīn 'Aṭṭār*. (Manchester University Press, 1976) pp. 30-31.

3   Atkinson, William Walker, and Three Initiates. "*The Kybalion (1908 Edition)*" Open Library, The Yogi Publication Society, 1 Jan. 1970, openlibrary. org/books/OL24669832M/The_Kybalion.

4   Ibid., pp. 26-28

5   Ibid., pp. 28-30

is aligned to a specific purpose and are masters of their purpose because they have learned how to intelligently move between two worlds, the known and the unknown.

The proceeding line, "Their father made them sit together one day. 'You are all', he said, 'conversant with the knowledge of the world,'" alludes to the third Hermetic principle, The Principle of Vibration. The Principle of Vibration teaches that nothing is at rest and that everything is in motion. It also dictates that one should control their mental vibration and know that they could also control others' mental vibrations.[6] 'Aṭṭār's image of the sons sitting together "conversant" with all worldly knowledge is a brilliant juxtaposition in that the uninitiated reader would perceive the sons as at rest, since they are sitting, while the initiated reader knows that this is a guise, for even though the sons are sitting, they are not at rest, since they are "conversant with the knowledge of the world," or thinking, vibrating with thought. The proceeding three lines continue The Principle of Vibration before moving seamlessly to the fourth Hermetic principle, The Principle of Polarity.

"One of the princes was the first to reveal his secret. 'It is related,' he said, 'by the great and eminent,'" declares The Principle of Polarity, evident in the key phrase "It is related." The Principle of Polarity teaches the well-known axiom, "opposites are the same, differing only in degree."[7] The simplest way to think of this principle would be to think of heat and cold: heat and cold, though considered opposites, are in fact the varying degrees of the same thing, temperature, as cold ascends into heat and heat descends into cold (as above, so below). The proceeding four lines continue The Principle of Polarity while the fifth and sixth serve as segways into the fifth Hermetic principle, The Principle of Rhythm.

---

6   See Atkinson, William Walker, and Three Initiates pp. 30-31
7   Ibid., pp. 32-35

"He that is near to the sun, how should he wish for a single beam? Such is my desire, and if I have it not, nothing but madness shall be my faith." Here, polarity meets rhythm in the "near to the sun." The initiate is now close to enlightenment but he must be certain that his action ("wish," "desire") aligns with *wish's* and *desire's* reaction ("if I have it not, nothing but madness"), as The Principle of Rhythm speaks to self-mastery and declares that there is always an action and a reaction, just as a pendulum swings back and forth, as tides ebb and flow, structures rise and fall, one lives then dies, etc.[8] In order to advance to the next stage of enlightenment through self-mastery, the initiate must, for lack of a better phrase, keep his eye on the prize and remain in rhythm to reach the true "perfection beyond this," which brings us to cause and effect.

The sixth Hermetic principle, The Principle of Cause and Effect, is revealed in the father's reply: "Beware of lust, for with lust thou art very drunk. When a man's heart is imprisoned in venery, all the coin of his being will be spent." The Principle of Cause and Effect is just that, and here it means be careful what you wish for and know from which state of mind you are wishing. Just as The Principle of Rhythm declares that every action has a reaction, The Principle of Cause and Effect declares that nothing happens by chance and that if the initiate has reached this stage of awareness, he is now a player in the game of life rather than a pawn in the game of life and that he can now use this principle, this Universal Law, rather than being used by it.[9] When one masters this principle, they then reach the seventh and final Hermetic principle, The Principle of Gender.

The closing lines thus declare The Principle of Gender: "But every woman who is manlike in her conduct is a complete stranger to such lust, [j]ust as that woman who was separated from her husband became the leader of men in the court of God." The Principle of Gender evokes the Hermetic hermaphrodite (Hermes-Aphrodite) and declares that gender

---

8   See Atkinson, William Walker, and Three Initiates pp. 35-38
9   Ibid., pp. 38-39

is present in everything on the physical, mental, and spiritual planes.[10] Hermetic *gender* refers to generation, regeneration, and creation, and this principle is the most obscure of all the

Hermetic principles. One could think of this principle as every thing or every person containing two elements: A human embryo begins at conception (creation), develops into a female (generation), then either remains a female or develops into a male (regeneration), but the male will always be part female since he was first created, or generated, as such. One could also consider the sun and moon, as the sun is often considered male and the moon often female, with one generating day, the other generating night, with both being reborn with each cycle, or regenerated, by the central source-point itself, Earth and its rotation. In this sense, one could also consider Earth as the ultimate Hermetic principle which embodies all Universal Laws, as Earth's ability to rotate serves as a prime example of self-mastery over that which is perfectly, eternally, generated. It is important to note, too, that the reader begins Discourse I at "One who had traveled the world but lost" and eventually arrives "in the court of God" by way of one father and six sons, or seven principles.

In a chapter titled "Religious Ideas and Alchemy," from *Psychology and Alchemy*, Carl Jung writes that true alchemical processes can only be achieved when practiced with perfect love (much like the Sufi path) as the alchemist is considered God's servant.[11] Jung continues:

The alchemical *opus* deals in the main not just with chemical experiments as such, but with something resembling psychic processes expressed in pseudochemical language ... A wealth of evidence accumulates to show that in alchemy there are two—in our eyes—heterogeneous currents flowing side by side[12] ... The

---

10 Ibid., pp. 39-41
11   Jung, C. G. *Collected Works of C.G. Jung, Volume 12: Psychology and Alchemy*. Translated by R. F. C. Hull, (Princeton University Press, 1980) p. 281.
12 Ibid., p. 258

alchemist is quite aware that he writes obscurely. He admits that he veils his meaning on purpose ... But cannot proclaim aloud just what the *prima materia* or the *lapis* is[13] ... All, from the very earliest times, have agreed that their art is sacred and divine, and likewise that their work can be completed only with the help of God ... The knowledge acquired may not be passed on to others unless they are worthy of it. Since all the essentials are expressed in metaphors they can be communicated only to the intelligent, who possess the gift of comprehension. The foolish allow themselves to be infatuated by literal interpretations and recipes, and fall into error. When reading the literature, one must not be content with just *one* book but must possess many books, for 'one book opens another.' Moreover one must read carefully, paragraph by paragraph; then one will make discoveries.[14]

I offer this quote by Jung to help validate Stepien's assertions regarding 'Aṭṭār's intentions and poetic motivations. My aforementioned deconstruction of Discourse I could of course be chalked-up to coincidence or personal subjectivity, since Sufi philosophy—like numerous other philosophies mentioned in this essay and throughout history—share the common trait of gathering around seven objectives. Comparatively expounding the significance of the number seven in relation to every spiritual philosophy throughout history would take far more pages than this one essay allows, and though I run the risk of presumption here, I must leave this be for now. That said, I believe that the first story of Discourse XIX, "Story of the beast called Halu," offers a more clear, compelling, definitive case of 'Aṭṭār's encoding Hermetic-alchemical principles into his poetry. I will now turn to the introduction and first story of Discourse XIX, offered below in its entirety, which I believe 'Aṭṭār encoded with the seven alchemical stages

---

13   Ibid., p. 295
14   See Jung, C. G. pp. 316-317

of transformation. In this deconstruction, I aim to show how 'Aṭṭār reveals to the reader each one of the seven alchemical principles in their respective order.

Discourse XIX

There came the sixth son, his heart filled with mysteries, raining pearls from the diamond of his tongue.

He said to the father: 'It is my constant desire to practise alchemy.

If I can acquire the science of alchemy, all the people of the world will turn to me for the philosopher's stone.

If I achieve that fortune I shall achieve faith also, for if I have the one I shall have the other.

By myself I shall fill the world with peace; I will make the poor rich.'
Father's reply

The father said to him: 'Thy heart is overcome with greed; therefore it is that it seeks the philosopher's stone.

What wouldst thou with this base world, this haunt of deceit and hatred?

For the world in an old hag with seven veils, having donned all seven to seduce thee.

I perceive that from greed thou hast lost all repose; thou art as restless as a bird caught in a snare.

For dust is the food on the bird of greed; only on dust does it ever eat its fill.'

(1) "Story of the beast called Halu"

'Ata, that man of Khorasan, says that there is a beast equal in size to a hundred mountains.

It dwells on the far side of the mountain called Qaf.

The name of that enormous beast is Halu, for it is a voracious eater.

In front of it are seven plains covered with grass; behind it there are seven seas within its reach.

It comes in the early morning and eats all the grass on the seven plains.

Having stripped in an instant the seven plains it drains in a single draught all the seven seas.

And having finished eating it cannot sleep a wink at night for worry and anxiety,

Thinking, "What shall I eat here tomorrow? I have eaten everything. What shall I do?"

But the next day the Almighty replenishes the plains and seas once again.—

Because man's greed is absolute, therefore God calls him Halu.

How is it that a spark of fire, wont to rear its head so high, bows down again when it touches a piece of wood?

If thou have in thee today a single a single spark of greed, it too will bow down in order to consume thee.

It is better therefore if thou knowest how to scatter water upon the fire.

Otherwise thou shalt be neither sober nor drunk but shalt remain a fire-worshipper for all eternity.

And if thou have ill-gotten goods to the extent of a single grain, for that

one grain thou shalt suffer eternal punishment.'[15]

The seven alchemical stages of transformation are often depicted as material metaphors for spiritual transformation, i.e., creating the Philosopher's Stone is a metaphor for attaining spiritual enlightenment. The seven alchemical stages of transformation contain within them the seven Hermetic principles: think of each as sharing one side of the same

---

15   See ʿAṭṭār, Farīd al-Dīn, and John Andrew Boyle pp. 278-279

coin. The names for these stages have been presented as various terms throughout history, most often in Latin, but for the sake of consistency here, I will refer to them in their respective order as follows: Calcination, Dissolution, Separation, Conjunction, Fermentation, Distillation, and Coagulation. In some contexts, there can be as little as four alchemical stages of transformation or as many as fourteen alchemical stages of transformation dependent upon the initiate's (or metallurgist's) goal, but the seven stages I present here are considered the most common and true-to-divine use, as gleaned from ancient Kemetic philosophy[16] and as allegedly uttered by the God Thoth and written by his initiates, long before Thoth was removed from his Kemetic and Egyptian roots and renamed the Hermes that we know today.

The "Story of the beast called Halu" is an alchemical poem. Each turn of the poem declares one of the seven alchemical stages of transformation. I include the prologue with "Story of the beast called Halu" here as evidence that 'Aṭṭār was priming the reader for their work ahead. 'Aṭṭār is doing his reader a favor here by writing, "'It is my constant desire to practise alchemy. If I can acquire the science of alchemy, all the people of the world will turn to me for the philosopher's stone." One must admit that 'Aṭṭār could not have stated his poetic intention any

---

16   "All the fundamental and basic teachings embedded in the esoteric teachings of every race may be traced back to Hermes. Even the most ancient teachings of India undoubtedly have their roots in the original Hermetic Teachings ... There may still be found a certain basic resemblance and correspondence which underlies the many and often quite divergent theories entertained and taught by the occultists of these different lands today. The student of Comparative Religions will be able to perceive the influence of the Hermetic Teachings in every religion worthy of the name." "Among these great Masters of Ancient Egypt there once dwelt one of whom Masters hailed as 'The Master of Masters.' This man, if 'man' indeed he was, dwelt in Egypt in the earliest days. He was known as Hermes Trismegistus. He was the father of the Occult Wisdom; the founder of Astrology; the discoverer of Alchemy." See Atkinson, William Walker, and Three Initiates pp. 8-9, pp. 14-15

clearer here. In this prologue, the word "alchemy" is mentioned twice and the term "philosopher's stone" is mentioned twice, and as we know, repetition in poetry is a signal to pay attention. It is important to note, too, that the prologue and "Story of the beast called Halu," together, mentions the word "seven" seven times, which is not coincidence.[17]

"Story of the beast called Halu" opens with the description of a beast the size of "a hundred mountains" who lives "on the far side of the mountain called Qaf," which tells us that the beast is not a physical beast rather a spiritual inclination or teaching lifted from the Quran, which reveals to us on the surface, and for the uninitiated readers of the time, that the story will walk us through the seven veils of Sufi philosophy; however, the initiated, or the ones called to alchemical initiation, are moved through Sufi philosophy while also being moved through alchemical philosophy, concurrently, recalling Jung's "heterogeneous currents flowing side by side." In front of Halu are seven plains within reach and behind Halu are seven seas within reach. One early morning, Halu eats all the grass on the seven plains then empties the seven seas due to thirst. Halu has eaten and drunk all that was available then thinks the question, "What shall I eat here tomorrow? What shall I do?" God then answers Halu's question by replenishing the grass and seas and Halu learns the hard lesson of greed.

"Early morning" alludes to the sunrise, and in alchemical symbology, the sun is a metaphor for *vitriol*—or the green lion, hence the mention of "grass" in the same line as "early morning"—and symbolizes the perfection of all matter, or that which creates gold/enlightenment. The lines, "eats all the grass on the seven plains" and "drains in a single draught all the seven seas" declare the first alchemical stage of transformation, Calcination. Alchemically, Calcination is the heating of the original substance, lead, into ash. Spiritually, this original substance is the *Prima Materia*, or aether, with Calcination referring to

---

17   I took the liberty of highlighting in bold the word "seven" as it appears throughout "Story of the beast called Halu" on page 9 of this essay.

the destruction of the ego and the detachment from worldly materials and desires which prevent one's spiritual growth or perfection. Thus, "eats all the grass on the seven plains" and "drains in a single draught all the seven seas" is the destruction of, or the emptying or depletion of, the original material in one fell swoop, an emptying which then requires the initiate to turn inward to God and ask, "What shall I do [now]?"

The next line, "the Almighty replenishes the plains and seas," declares the second alchemical stage of transformation, Dissolution. Alchemically, Dissolution is the act of dissolving the ashes of Calcination in water. Spiritually, Dissolution refers to one's rediscovering the rejected parts of their identity that have been hidden or veiled by ego. Dissolution teaches the initiate that they must consciously omit control over their identity, thus the replenishment of the plains and seas here refers to the spiritually-cleansing act of replenishing by first dissolving.

The proceeding lines, "a spark of fire ... a piece of wood ... a single spark of greed ... it too will bow down in order to consume thee," declares the third alchemical stage of transformation, Separation. Alchemically and spiritually, Separation is the filtration and isolation of the remnants of Dissolution and the discarding of the remnants that no longer serve one's goal, i.e., one will discover their true essence in the remaining remnants. Thus, "a spark of fire" and "a piece of wood" are worthy remnants, while "a single spark of greed" is a remnant that, if the initiate chooses to not discard, will prevent him from moving forward on his path toward enlightenment.

The next line, "It is better therefore if thou knowest how to scatter water upon the fire," declares the fourth alchemical stage of transformation, Conjunction. Alchemically, Conjunction is the recombination of the remaining chosen remnants of Separation in the aim of creating a new material substance. Spiritually, Conjunction is the recombination of the remaining chosen elements of Separation in the aim of forming a new spiritual element, to merge the now purer unconscious with the now purer consciousness. Thus, "scatter water upon the fire" creates a new element, smoke, which can only occur by combining the two aforementioned worthy remnants—the "fire" and "wood" from Separation—which leads directly into the fifth alchemical stage of transformation, Fermentation.

Fermentation is evidenced in the next line, "Otherwise thou shalt be neither sober nor drunk but shalt remain a fire-worshipper for all eternity." This declares that if the initiate does not choose the aforementioned remnants wisely, he will be stuck in a state of spiritual limbo as a "fire-worshipper" and will forever watch the flame "rear its head" and "bow down" and nothing more, since at this stage, the initiate now knows too much to return to a state of blissful ignorance but does not yet know enough to be in a state of drunken love. The key words here are "sober" and "drunk," which while on the surface represent the Sufi symbology of the words, also directly refer to Fermentation. Alchemically, Fermentation is the introduction of living organisms into the new substance. Spiritually, Fermentation teaches intuition, inspired action, and divine intervention achieved through deep prayer and meditation.

The first half of the next line, "and if thou have ill-gotten goods to the extent of a single grain," declares the sixth alchemical stage of transformation, Distillation. Alchemically, Distillation is the boiling and condensation of the fermented substance in the aim of purifying the substance, similar to how alcohol is made by distilling a fermenting "grain." Spiritually, Distillation is the ultimate freeing of ego and emotion, which leads to a truer perception of reality. Thus, if an initiate has even "a single grain" of "ill-gotten goods," they are not truly free from ego and emotion and cannot fully perceive reality in its purest state.

The second half of the last line, "for that one grain thou shalt suffer eternal punishment," declares the seventh and final alchemical stage of transformation, Coagulation. Alchemically, Coagulation represents the distilled substance in its final crystallized form, or gold. The initiate who began his journey as proverbial lead in stage one would have successfully completed his journey at the end of stage seven and would now be considered enlightened, or goldened—if the previous Distillation was indeed pure and without "a single grain"—as the knowledge of all seven alchemical stages of transformation is what constitutes the singular Philosopher's Stone. Spiritually, Coagulation is the attainment of divine union and the embodiment of a self-aware spirit, or, enlightenment.

Further, it is important to note that the pace in which 'Attār reveals the seven alchemical stages of transformation mirrors the pace in which an alchemical metallurgist would need to work in order to successfully turn lead to gold. This is evidenced in the pacing of the story and in the locations of the encoded first five alchemical stages of transformation, as these five stages require time in an alchemist's laboratory, whereas the last two stages appear as condensed metaphors at the end of the text, sharing only one line, similar to how material coagulation rapidly occurs following the removal of fire from that which is being distilled. As Stepien writes:

> Order prevails in the cosmos ... This order is the manifestation of the divine presence in the cosmos. 'Attār then observes that order (in this case, of words harmoniously arranged)[18] ... The ordered perfection of the Creator is reflected in the order of Its created world ... The ordered perfection of poetry reflects that of the poet: to the extent that he is himself perfect ... To the extent that he embodies divine perfection in his poetry ... To the extent that his poetry embodies the divine secrets and mysteries[19] ... For the mystic-poet ... submit[s] his will completely to the divine imperatives of the religious law and, consequently, is able to hear the poetry and transmit it from the divine dictate.[20]

---

18   See Stepien, Rafal p. 93
19   See Stepien, Rafal p. 98
20   Ibid., p. 106

While I have analyzed the ways in which 'Aṭṭār encodes the seven alchemical stages of transformation and the seven Hermetic principles into the Sufi philosophies of Discourse I and Discourse XIX, it is important to note that the alchemist, the Philosopher's Stone, and the alchemical processes of spiritual and metallurgic transmutation are mentioned quite often throughout a number of other discourses in 'Aṭṭār's *Book of God*: clearly in Discourse XX and most notably in Discourse XXI and Discourse XXII. In Discourse XXI, 'Aṭṭār writes: "If thou wouldst achieve perfection in love thou must be perpetually in three conditions: First weeping, secondly burning, and thirdly bleeding"[21] which I believe alludes to the *Tria Prima*, or the three principles of alchemy, the three alchemy primes[22] (Salt, Sulphur, Mercury): "weeping" represents Salt, "burning" represents Sulphur, and "bleeding" represents Mercury. In Discourse XXII, in "Story of the deer from which musk is produced," when discussing the practice of alchemy, 'Aṭṭār writes, quite glaringly: "It is best if this secret remains hidden."[23] And perhaps it is. Perhaps the coveted Philosopher's Stone works best when hidden, in poetry, and here in 'Aṭṭār's poetic discourses, in a book befittingly titled *Book of God*.

---

21   See 'Aṭṭār, Farīd al-Dīn, and John Andrew Boyle p. 303

22   See Goodrick-Clarke, Nicholas. "DAS BUCH PARAGRANUM (1529-30)" PARACELSUS, (Stanford University, web.stanford.edu/class/history13/Readings/clarke.htm) par. 6.

23   See 'Aṭṭār, Farīd al-Dīn, and John Andrew Boyle p. 333

References

Atkinson, William Walker, and Three Initiates. *"The Kybalion (1908 Edition)"* Open Library, The Yogi Publication Society, 1 Jan. 1970, openlibrary.org/books/OL24669832M/The_Kybalion.

'Aṭṭār, Farīd al-Dīn, and John Andrew Boyle. *The Ilahi-Nama, or, Book of God of Farid Al-Dīn 'Aṭṭār.* Manchester University Press, 1976.

Goodrick-Clarke, Nicholas. *"DAS BUCH PARAGRANUM (1529-30)"* PARACELSUS, Stanford University, web.stanford.edu/class/history13/Readings/clarke.htm

Jung, C. G. *Collected Works of C.G. Jung, Volume 12: Psychology and Alchemy.* Translated by R. F. C. Hull, Princeton University Press, 1980.

Stepien, Rafal. "A Study in Sufi Poetics: The Case of 'Aṭṭār Nayshābūrī." Oriens, vol. 41, no. 1/2, 2013, pp. 77–120.

On the Mythopoetics of
Holy Hearing and Holy Seeing

In this essay, I will aim to incorporate two of Thomas B. Coburn's methods of examination of Hindu scripture and Hindu Word into my study of mythopoetics to better the understanding of how mythopoetics functions in the realm of spiritual experience and holy hearing, using the term *spiritual experience* over *religious experience* to better incorporate modes and practices that cannot be defined as *religious*. Coburn's two methods of examination that I will incorporate here are the primacy of experience and the ontology of language; and the sociology of language and the power of holy hearing. The term *mythopoetics* can provoke a broad spectrum of interpretation, so I will employ it here to mean any divine, bio-mythic, or poetically-charged experience that proves to reveal its full self, or full sacredness, through the language or text by which it is shared with others. I will explore the ways in which mythopoetics can be positioned in agreement with Coburn's "writtenness" while seeking ways in which mythopoetics functions as a spiritual practice that is fueled by ontological motivations charged by the urgency of the language of holy hearing and holy seeing. Coburn situates the term *holy hearing* to mean the literal outward hearing of a sacred word or sound, and I will expand the term here to mean inner holy hearing, as well; e.g., hearing a wholly original sacred word or sound in either a dream, hypnagogic state, hypnopompic state, or meditative state that then acts as a catalyst for a divinely-inspired poem to later be written then given or uttered to others by the poet-hearer or seer, deemed sacred in its experience by both the poet-hearer or seer and her or his readers or listeners. I define the terms "poem" and "poetry" in this essay to mean any ancient, modern, or contemporary symbolic expression that holds the subjective power to proclaim, interpret, activate, or trigger religious or spiritual thought and experience in those who either approach it or are approached by it, resulting in individual phenomena, social phenomena, or both. I will also remove the term *scripture* here from any religious affiliation, thus employing its reference under one of its allied meanings, *holy writ*, in thinking of the divinely-inspired written poem.

In his essay, "'Scripture' in India: Towards a Typology of the Word in Hindu Life," Thomas B. Coburn seeks to understand features of Hindu scripture through a typology of the Word as evidenced in Hindu life. The problem for Coburn lies in the term *scripture*. Though the Word is in scripture, Coburn asserts that the Word is greater than scripture since *scripture* provokes a "writtenness" that conceals important features of holy words, thus declaring that Hindu holiness does not fully reside in its texts rather the oral and auric fields in which Hindu holiness operates (much in accord with Tazim R. Kassam's desire to reframe how *scripture* is interpreted and approached in regard to the Koran). As Coburn writes:

> [An] expectation of "writtenness" may mask certain important features of how holy words have been operative in human history: they have been oral/aural realities at least as much as they have been written ones, and the way that they have found their way into human lives is not through the eye, but through the ear. To argue the contrary is but to admit that we are heirs of Gutenberg, for the very notion of silent, individualized reading is scarcely known prior to the advent of the printing press. (Coburn 436-437)

Coburn locates a central dynamic of Hindu behavior towards the Word as *scripture*: the desire to preserve and write a text and the desire to understand spiritual ideas that are presented orally. In order to conceptualize an adequate approach to the study of the Word in relation to scripture, Coburn proposes that scholars examine three key topics, the two of necessity here being the primacy of experience and the ontology of language; and the sociology of language and the power of holy hearing. (Coburn's third key topic—the dialectic between the double Hindu terms *sruti* and *smrti*—is omitted here in this essay as I endeavor to approach mythopoetics as a practice belonging to a general individual and not to a specific culture.) To concretize his reasoning, Coburn offers five key aspects of Hindu religious life that distinguish the Word from scripture: Hindus have captured the Word verbatim; Hindus have treated certain stories as normative; Hindus have composed commentaries to make the Word accessible to modernity; Hindus have generated imitations of the Word; and Hindus have added to the embodiment of the Word over time. (Similarly, one could recall here how Leela Prasad aims to bring performative studies to ethical inquiry by calling on oral-literary criticisms that would allow ethnographic interpretations to remain fluid, as Prasad questions normative practices and ethnographic understandings which have failed to delineate narratives of individual experience within the poetics of tradition embedded in daily Hindu life.)

If *scripture* contains the essence of a living phenomenology of a holiness that cannot fully express its existence through the written language in which it seeks to exist, through what lens could one view *scripture* to better gauge the organic expressions of spiritual thought? Coburn's ontological approach to the Word and scripture helps answer this question when asked from within the frame of mythopoetics. Mythopoetics is typically studied through the lens of language viewed through the subjective lens of experience, and though the study of mythopoetics through an ontological lens could be considered just as subjective, Coburn's method of examination brings unique modes of approach to the timeworn adage of the poet writing to the divine in that he positions spiritual experience, language, and holy hearing as distinctive yet equally intrinsic parts of the whole. In other words, to fully understand the experience of a divinely inspired poem one must understand how language relates to the urgency of the experience from which the poem was born. As Gaston Bachelard states: "Poetry puts language in a state of emergence, in which life becomes manifest through its vivacity. These linguistic impulses, which stand out from the ordinary rank of pragmatic language, are miniatures of the vital impulse"

(Bachelard xxvii). The vital impulse is urgency and the dynamic life of language therein.

Coburn examines how words that come into existence through holy hearing or holy seeing are used to conceptualize the experience of their appearance, thus revealing with each proper use of the word the cosmic truth present within the human being who is hearing or seeing. Coburn expounds how these words are applied to the metaphors of hearing and seeing and explains how the metaphors used to contain the meanings of the words are intentionally positioned to bear the intense organic nature of their awarenesses, metaphors of apotheosis which elevate the human nature of their experience to the divine; i.e., the very existence and experience of these words prove themselves divine. In relation to poetry and the poet, Coburn cites Dutch Indologist Jan Gonda:

> [The Indian aestheticians] were of the opinion that the experiences of the poet, representing the hero of his work and that of the listener, reader, or, in general employer of the work are identical ... This consciousness of the presence of truth, of the divine, of the eternal or ultimate reality in a work of art which has been created by a truly inspired artist, together with the almost universal belief that words, especially duly formulated and rhythmically pronounced words, are bearers of power ... They are not made but "seen" by those men who have had the privilege of direct contact with divinity or the supra-mundane. (Coburn 442)

One could argue that a "privilege of direct contact with divinity" is not a privilege rather an experience that any human being is capable of acquiring, but this would miss the point. In mythopoetics, it is not the hearer or seer who is privileged (though they are certainly considered privileged by some), it is the product of the encounter, the poem itself, that is privileged—the poem as it first appears and is then born into the world to be recited, heard, and seen by others, its encounter both expansive and relational—thus a mythopoetic or divinely-inspired poem privileges others to connect with the same divine source or essence thereof from whence it came. From an ontological standpoint, one must argue that a divinely inspired poem can only be deemed divine if each person who reads or hears the poem feels divinely inspired. When it comes to definitional work, this may be true; however, if only one person reading or hearing a poem feels that it is divinely inspired, if they believe that reading or experiencing the poem has shifted their consciousness into a space of divine experience, then the poem did act as a catalyst for a divine experience to take place in that individual. Divine inspiration and divine experience are two sides of the same coin—one cannot exist without positioning itself onto the space of the other, for divine experience results in divine inspiration and vice versa, whether only in one individual (the poet) or between two or more individuals through space or time (between the poet and the individuals who later come to experience the poem).

To offer a personal narrative of poetic events here, to place this study in conversation with the good work: As a poet and reader, I have noticed that poetry often arrives to me in auspicious ways. I would say to others that this kind of poetry, or poem, if it's one I am to write, "found me," in some particular place, at some particular moment, through some cosmic or divine personal-poetic purpose as a hearer and seer. Though opening a door to a conversation on the levels of divinity in mythopoetic experience would be too great a task for this brief essay, I believe it is necessary to offer a poem in which I can better anchor my aforementioned conjectures regarding holy hearing and holy seeing to better understand Coburn's primacy of experience and ontology of language in relation to mythopoetics, or at least to my mythopoetics. That written, I will attempt to deconstruct a poem by nineteenth-century Nicaraguan poet Ruben Darío, which I am called to offer in its entirety:

SEASHELL (CARACOL)

On the beach I found a golden seashell.
It was massive and studded with fine pearls.
Europa stroked it with divine fingers
as she rode waves on a celestial bull.

With my lips, I played the shell's melody.
Deep in the azure mines of its whispers,
it told me about its secret treasures
under the echoing sea's reveille.

The salt pervades me in a bitter breeze,
and while the stars blessed Jason's reveries,
it swelled the Argonaut's white sails. I start

to hear the murmuring waves speak inside
the cryptic winds and the most profound tide ...
(The shell was formed in the shape of a heart.) (Darío 13)

"Seashell (Caracol)" is not only an example of sharp poetic craft but a brilliant example of a mythopoetic poem. Though "Seashell (Caracol)" speaks to a seashell as the object that one physically discovers and holds, it speaks more to the essence of the symbol of the seashell in its moment of literal or figurative finding; the symbolic, or mythic, perspective of the physical thing is what made the poem worth writing. Its urgency is present tense. One can hear "the shell's melody" as it sings through the line "under the echoing sea's reveille." Darío equates the aesthetic of the seashell to that of a moon goddess's once-touched treasure that emulates secret wisdom, triggering a direct mythopoetic response to a communion of one's Self with nature and to that which gives life and death (or transcendence) to both. In the symbol of the seashell one finds the sea—a meditative, creative, destructive force—which speaks to Darío's personal life. Fleeting moments, the ebb and flow of inner peace and storm, life's intricate balances are felt strongly in the last two stanzas. The poet holds tight the beauty (essence) of the seashell while acknowledging the "bitter breeze" and "cryptic winds" that surround, but then closes with the important parenthetical note, "The shell was formed in the shape of a heart." Darío demonstrates a "common rhythm" (holy hearing as felt within the body through its music) in this poem, a rhythm of the essence of the symbol of divine experience expounded by the urgency or primacy of the language of experience needing to actualize the symbol of itself through the poet's language. The poet *sees* the Argonaut's white sails and *envisions* Europa, not on the ocean in front of him but rather in his mind as the images of "holy seeing" within the poem's revelation. Darío's "holy seeing" is the ontological motivation behind the language of his experience, the language of the poem being more than just "written."

Coburn writes that "holy words ... must be seen alongside other transforming, sacramental activities, such as ... the worship of the divine in image form" (Coburn 444). The seashell of Darío's poem is the divine in image form, and Darío worshipped this divinity by writing the poem, thus the divinity remains charged for the reader.

When one reads "Seashell (Caracol)," one could feel as if they too are worshipping the divine through the image of Darío's seashell, or one could not. Just as Coburn highlights the propensity for Hindus to memorize and recite holy words as a manifestation (Coburn 447), I have memorized this poem and recite lines from it to myself often. Coburn states that "holiness of the Word is intrinsic ... one participates in it, not by understanding, but by hearing and reciting it" (Coburn 447), thus one continues to understand a divinely-inspired poem by hearing and reciting it. If you the reader have never read one poem, I would wager that you have at least heard and know of the phrase *two roads diverged in a yellow wood*. Though "The Road Not Taken" by Robert Frost has never triggered a divine experience in me personally, it has certainly triggered and continues to trigger a transcendent experience in many as it has become a poetically-charged Word or scripture in itself, a literary apotheosis that continues to live and move throughout popular mainstream American culture more than a century after it was penned, for example: In 2014, the poem became the inspiration for a video game titled Road Not Taken—a puzzle game about surviving life's surprises—and Frost's celebrated opening line, "Two roads diverged in a yellow wood," was spoken by a male voice-over artist in a commercial for the video game that same year. This is mythopoetics at work and a ripe example of Coburn's sociology of language and the power of holy hearing in contemporary mainstream American culture. Even if one does not wish to hear or remember *two roads diverged in a yellow wood*, one does hear and remember it because it continues to permeate our society through its own transcendental mythopoetic power.

The sociology of language and the power of holy hearing and holy seeing in relation to mythopoetics can also be found in the phrase *there is a man cut in two by the window*. In 1924, famed French writer and poet André Breton writes in his *Manifestoes of Surrealism* that this phrase arrived to him one night while in a hypnagogic state as a visual claircognizant flash in his mind (Breton 21). Breton immediately began to obsess over the phrase and eventually deduced that *there is a man cut in two by the window* meant that two realities could converge into one, that both the conscious and subconscious realms of experience could coexist simultaneously as a *surreality*. This phrase—this holy seeing of a line of language—was the catalyst for Breton to help establish and lead the Surrealist movement of the early-twentieth century, thus meaning that everything that was born from the Surrealist movement, including that which still continues to this day, can be linked to the ontological motivation behind *there is a man cut in two by the window*. Breton trusted that his *seeing* was a divine experience, and from that trust, the intellectual world was forever changed. I include Breton's experience here because Coburn calls on scholars to "rethink some of our familiar patterns of thought ... or the double desideratum of literally preserving and dynamically recreating the Word" (Coburn 447) when studying or defining aspects of the typology of the Word, and I believe that it is necessary to expand Coburn's notion to include other spaces in which the typology of the Word is often overlooked. Breton, too, calls on the reader to rethink their familiar patterns of thought:

> To you who write, these elements are, on the surface, *as strange to you as they are to anyone else*, and naturally you are wary of them. Poetically speaking, what strikes you about them above all is their *extreme degree of immediate absurdity*, the quality of this absurdity, upon closer scrutiny, being to give way to everything admissible, everything legitimate in the world: the disclosure of a certain number of properties and of facts no less objective, in the final analysis, than the others. (Breton 24)

Coburn calls on scholars to understand the *desire* to understand religious ideas that are presented verbally, but with Breton's experience in mind, one could expand this request to also include the desire to understand spiritual ideas that are presented verbally through holy seeing. One should consider *there is a man cut in two by the window* a holy hearing as well as a holy seeing since the sight was not that of a symbol but of a string of words that presented and charged themselves with an energy of desiring to be written, demystified, exalted and then born into the world as a literary and artistic movement. Coburn urges scholars to "think of the basic unit for discussing the … situation as the verbal utterance of a particular individual at a particular point in time … we have to proceed to such an extreme 'atomizing' of the material. More abstract approaches, based on prevailing conceptualizations, get us into difficulties" (Coburn 451). Mythopoetics, like the Word, is a "larger-than-scriptural phenomenon" (Coburn 454) that requires an "extreme atomizing of [its] material." Though the study of mythopoetics is often compartmentalized into various subfields—such as the sacral elements of poetic experience here—it may be necessary to approach the field as a theoretical cornerstone for the study of the phenomenal, for without the aforementioned phenomena, the foundational or normative frame of vision within this field would not exist and its compartmentalized parts would continue to be scattered throughout the forgotten meadow of scholarly concern. One could recall here *History and Presence* by Robert Orsi, as Orsi thoroughly explores the value in recognizing the nature of "real" presence, the presence of the gods and divinities that sustain religious and spiritual thought and practice. Orsi writes how presence requires absence and deduces that absence is authoritative while presence is a human norm, declaring that the challenge for all is to *see* the gods. In citing examples of the excess of religious expression—if one could consider poetry an excess of religious expression—Orsi states that "the critics fail to see that excess itself is the meaning" (Orsi 57), thus the product itself contains the meaning, i.e., the poem contains the poet's myth. Ruben Darío recognized the "real" presence of divinity in "Seashell (Caracol)," just as André Breton recognized the "real" presence of divinity in *there is a man cut in two by the window*, with the latter leading to a surrealism that thrived by pouring its symbols of psychic excess into the presence of a reality framed by the absence of rationality. Breton's *there is a man cut in two by the window* and Frost's *two roads diverged in a yellow wood* have successfully positioned themselves as mythopoetic social phenomena within their respected social realities.

One must now consider Émile Durkheim's sociological method of approach in relation to the mythopoetics of holy hearing and holy seeing. Durkheim's sociological method of approach—founded upon a functionalist perspective and rooted in an ontological commitment to the reality of social phenomena—positions social reality as an intrinsic dualistic phenomenon that circulates between and within the individual and society, conceptualizing the individual and society as synergistic systems of forces which in and of themselves offer distinguished ways of interpreting how the collective consciousness affects individual consciousness in respect to religion, religious or spiritual thought, and religious or spiritual life. Durkheim insists that "primitive" religions share essential traits with modern religions, traits that are social and produced by collective thought. In *The Elementary Forms of Religious Life*, Durkheim seeks to uncover the true religious nature of humankind—the origin of religious thought—in the hope of better understanding modern religions. Durkheim asserts that in order to do this, one must first unearth a fundamental aspect of humankind's religious nature by studying an archaic or "primitive" religion; e.g., a religion that is wholly original and self-contained. Durkheim posits that the religious phenomena of these religions still offer visible marks of their origins and aims to uncover these origins by isolating the constituent elements of these religions in the belief that historical interpretations have long repressed or replaced the original interpretations:

> At the foundation of all systems of beliefs and cults, there must necessarily be a certain number of fundamental representations and modes of ritual conduct that, despite the diversity of forms that the one and the other may have taken on, have the same objective meaning everywhere and everywhere fulfill the same functions. It is these enduring elements that constitute what is eternal and human in religion. They are the whole objective content of the idea that is expressed when *religion* in general is spoken of. (Durkheim 4)

One constituent element of what is eternal and human in religion is the expression of symbol through language, while poetry is one fundamental mode of ritual conduct. Poetry was born from humankind's religious nature, and in a number of cases, the explanatory power within poetry (or sacred texts deemed poetic) helped to create religion itself. We know that there is not one religion that does not call on the expression of symbol in some way, shape, or form to amplify or embed its meaning within an individual or collective consciousness. Durkheim writes: "Social life, in all its aspects and in every period of its history, is made possible only by a vast symbolism" (Durkheim 231). Poetry represents one way in which societies throughout history have penetrated, possessed, and redefined the symbols of their experience, thus deeming mythopoetic the *holy writ* poetry that was inspired by holy hearing or holy seeing. Durkheim continues: "We must know how to reach beneath the symbol to grasp the reality it represents and that gives the symbol its true meaning" (Durkheim 2). Durkheim's view that language is developed by society is relevant here because it links individual expression of symbol to collective assimilation of symbol. Without symbol, there would be no poems or mythopoetics therein in which a shift of consciousness could result, since the symbol is what enables the hearer or seer (or reader) to appropriate the poetic or divine experience as their own.

Though fundamentally individual and subjective, how do the symbols of a momentary state of a particular consciousness—as experienced in the making of poetry when reflecting on definite objects—actualize themselves as resolute elements in religious practices and belief systems that span centuries? They actualize themselves through the mythopoetics of an immediate language charged by ontological motivation, and as Durkheim suggests, and as Coburn would likely agree, one could expound an answer to this question by studying the poetry of "primitive" religions. Paul Ricœur writes beautifully to the matter:

There is no symbolism prior to man who speaks, even though the power of symbols is rooted more deeply, in the expressiveness of the cosmos, in what desire wants to say, in the varied image-contents that men have. But in each case it is in language that the cosmos, desire, and the imaginary achieve speech ... thus it is the poet who shows us the birth of the word, in its hidden form in the enigmas of the cosmos and of the psyche. The power of the poet is to show forth symbols at the moment of when poetry places language in a state of emergence. (Ricœur 16)

With Durkheim and Coburn in mind, one is compelled to seek the origins of mythopoetics by asking: What is the first socially adopted symbol that appeared through holy hearing or holy seeing that poetry placed in a state of emergence which later became a mythopoetic social phenomenon within its respected social reality? If a society agrees that a certain flower exists, even if the flower has never been seen by the individuals of that society, then that flower becomes a symbol of that society's collective consciousness on which certain experiences attach themselves. Let us take for example the Christian cross. If one reads or writes a poem about the Christian cross, it is likely that the poem will speak more to the feeling, embodiment, or disembodiment of the Christ-consciousness rather than that of the wooden object, since the symbol of the Christian cross transcends all aspects of its physical representation as it is a socially adopted symbol of a divinity embedded in the collective consciousness of our social reality, making the Christian cross itself a mythopoetic symbol. Durkheim states that "a sensation or an image is always linked to a definite object or collection of definite objects, and it expresses the momentary state of a particular consciousness" (Durkheim 13). In *Philosophy, Literature, and Politics: Essays Honoring Ellis Sandoz*, Charles Embry expounds on the mythopoetic symbol:

One part of man's response to the experience of reality is to articulate its significance, and this he does through the creation of symbols that represent experience and its underlying reality. Symbols are "the language phenomena engendered by the process of participatory experience." There is "a plurality of symbolisms that man has employed, including myth, revelation, science, philosophy, and poetry." (Embry 149)

Once a symbol is created and deemed a representation of a person's experience, it carries with it a mythopoetic responsibility not only to the society in which the person belongs but to the other societies in which the symbol may come to root. It seems that Embry would agree with Coburn's primacy of experience, Durkheim's collective assimilation of symbol, and Ricœur's assertions on symbol in relation to poetry and what *desire* "wants to say." Here, Embry expounds the significance of recognizing mythopoetic symbols as distinct:

> Mythopoetic symbolism may be actually superior to its philosophical heir. The three points I want to consider are these: first, mythopoetic symbolization is not as susceptible to "ideological deformation" as is philosophy. Second, poetic symbols are more comprehensive than philosophical symbols. Finally, poetry invites openness to experience and an opportunity for enacted experience that philosophy does not. (Embry 151)

In thinking of Coburn calling on scholars to understand the *desire* to understand religious ideas that are presented verbally while recalling Ricœur's "what desire wants to say," one must now ponder whether or not *desire* could be considered the language of the social performance of symbol while questioning if a symbolic language of social performance would even exist within a society that was not ontologically motivated to become more rooted to the cosmos through mythopoetic experience, for there cannot be a social phenomenon within a social reality if the social phenomena did not first *desire* to emerge from within its social reality.

References

Bachelard, Gaston. *The Poetics of Space*. Penguin Books, 2014.

Breton, André, and Richard Seaver. *Manifestoes of Surrealism*. Univ. of Mich. Press, 1969.

Coburn, Thomas B. "'Scripture' in India: Towards a Typology of the Word in Hindu Life." *Journal of the American Academy of Religion*, vol. 52, no. 3, 1984, pp. 435–459. JSTOR, www.jstor.org/stable/1464202.

Darío Rubén. *Selected Writings*. Penguin, 2006.

Durkheim, Émile, et al. *The Elementary Forms of the Religious Life*. George Allen and Unwin Ltd, 1976.

Embry, Charles R., et al. *Philosophy, Literature, and Politics: Essays Honoring Ellis Sandoz*. University of Missouri Press, 2005.

Orsi, Robert A. *History and Presence*. Belknap Harvard, 2018.

Ricœur, Paul. *Freud and Philosophy: An Essay on Interpretation*. Yale University Press, 1977.

Acknowledgments

Praise be to God, for everything, for saving me from the very real and very spiritual hell my life became during the writing of this book. I should not be here today, but I am because of Him.

Thank you to my grandma, Barbara Jane Dailey, for bestowing upon me the theology that would ultimately prove detrimental to my salvation. How you've spent your life walking the good path is an absolute testament to His glory. Thank you for teaching me how to stay vigilant of the fire on all sides.

Thank you to my father, Kip Sheets, for being all that he was, "warts and all." Dad, it wasn't until after you passed that I learned things about you that I now see in myself, important things. You are a mirror to me in many ways, and I know you'd be okay with the truths I wrote in "A New Fire" because they are exactly that—true. If only I'd known then, though, what I know now, what I have experienced since. Thank you for all that you tried so hard to do. I see you, now. I'm proud to be your son.

Thank you to my Brothers and Sisters at Lexington Primitive Baptist Church. You are Light.

Thank you to Harvard Divinity School's Chandra Mohammed and Diane Moore for inviting me so thoughtfully into discussion spaces over this past year. Deep gratitude and appreciation.

Thank you to Terry Tempest Williams for inspiring me to write truths for a general readership. The creative nonfiction essays that comprise the "Narratives" section of this book were written in Spring 2021 while enrolled as a student in her course, Finding Beauty in a Broken World.

Thank you to The Poetry Foundation for featuring "Lime Tree" and "A True Dimension of Nothingness" in the March 2024 issue of POETRY.

"Encounter" first appeared in *Modern Language Studies* (MLS), in affiliation with the Modern Language Association (MLA), Winter 2025. Thank you to editor Patrick Henry for supporting this bit of work/philosophy.

Thank you to Lydialyle Gibson at *Harvard Magazine* for inviting me to write the homeless essay, but more important, for keeping a necessary conversation going.

Thank you to each prize, grant, and fellowship committee member that has spent time reading and considering my various applications this year, for the energy you gave and continue to give to reading and considering my work and research. (Without you, an engine would stall.)

To the April Gloaming Publishing team, to the hands and hearts that labor to deliver my books to the world book and book again— Thank You. You are more appreciated than you know.

To Lance Ümmenhofer and Robyn Leigh Lear: I will never cease to make known that you have believed in my work since Day 1. It has been an absolute joy, and honor, to work with you over these past eight years—and we've only just begun. I am beyond proud to be in literary and creative community with you. Here's to every gift, and every burden, the good work bestows and requires of us.

Thank you to the spirit of Poetry for giving me my next book-in-progress, *Nova Qua Nova*. I did not expect to arrive, at the near-middle of my career, to the task of having to craft a 400-page book of quatrains, but here we are. Us poets are but servants to the work.

(Oh, how I love this wild lineage . . .)

And thank you, reader, for being here. This book, like any book, is a dead thing when not opened. Thank you for bringing it to life here. I hope that something in here has read you back.

About the Author

Jason Adam Sheets comes from a lineage of Appalachian musicians, songwriters, poets, and preachers. He earned a Master's of Theological Studies in Theopoetics from Harvard Divinity School, where he recently served as a Teaching Fellow. His research focuses on how poetic language works to evoke religious experience. Sheets' commitment to the field can be seen in his work as a poet and essayist. Books include *V Verse Is I* (AGP, 2025), *A Madness of Blue Obsidian* (AGP, 2022), *The Hour Wasp* (AGP, 2017), and *Theopoetica: An Anthology* (AGP, 2022). New poems appear in *POETRY* (March, 2024) and *Modern Language Studies* (Winter, 2025). A Pushcart Prize nominee, his writing was recently featured in *Harvard Magazine* and by Oxford University's Research Centre in the Humanities. He teaches for Poetry in America, in affiliation with the eponymous PBS television series and in conjunction with the National Education Equity Lab, and has worked as a writing and publishing mentor for AWP's Writer to Writer mentorship program. His work has been supported by Harvard University, PEN America, *Poets & Writers Magazine*, and Mass Cultural Council.

Comparable April Gloaming Titles

A Madness of Blue Obsidian by Jason Adam Sheets

The Hour Wasp by Jason Adam Sheets

The Wolf Can Smell This is My Acre by Klyd Watkins

clawing at the grounded moon by Darren C. Demaree

All Things Holy and Heathen by Chelsea C. Jackson

Love Letters from an Arsonist by David van den Berg

The Wingtip Prophecy by Brent House

Dear Excavator by Evan D. Williams